"Ben's gritty but at times light-hearted description of his time in Afghanistan is surely one that will resonate with all service members who have answered the call to deploy for their country. *20 Year Letter* is a must-read for veterans, military families, and anyone who truly wants to see a window into the world of our brave men and women serving overseas."

—COL Brad Wenstrup
USAR, Member, US House of Representatives

"Well reasoned and well written, with *20-Year Letter* Ben Warner expertly captures the sights, sounds, pain, pleasure and pride of an early deployment to Afghanistan. No matter where or when you deployed, Ben's tale will bring you back to your time in a combat theater. I highly recommend this very enjoyable read for all that have served and those that support us!"

—Richard J. Gallant
Major General, Retired, USA

"One of the most powerful books I have read in a quite some time. These are the stories of a young soldier developing into a senior leader of others. Here you will learn about the author's time in training, and most of all his time in combat in the lethal cauldron of the mountains of Afghanistan. You will get a cold-grip reality of what it's like to meet a comrade and a friend that may not be there the next day. I couldn't put it down."

—Nathan Aguinaga
Master Sergeant, Retired, USA, and Author of *Division: Life on Ardennes Street, Roster Number Five-Zero,* and *Wake Up, You're Having Another Nightmare*

"Ben Warner delivers a no-nonsense, no-holds-barred memoir of his 2002 Army deployment in *20-Year Letter: An Afghanistan Chronicle*. Memories fade over time . . . unless those memories are forged during a combat deployment. Like your first sweetheart kiss, you'll never forget the first kiss of combat service. Almost twenty years later, Ben's description of events, feelings, and consequences he endured during his Afghanistan duty remains as vivid today as if these happened just last week.

"*20-Year Letter: An Afghanistan Chronicle* offers intimate details of military service which will touch the hearts of veterans, but will be eye-opening for civilian readers. Veterans will laugh, cry, and shake their heads knowingly, while civilians will gain a greater appreciation and understanding of the military mindset. Put this book on your 'to-read' list."

—Kelly Galvin
CPT, Retired, USA, Author of *PowerPoint Ranger: My Iraq War Logs*

"Stand in line. Fantasize about hot food. Strategize about trips to the commode. Get irrationally excited about cold soda. This is the *real* military, which Ben describes so well. An honest, engaging depiction of deployed military life, where the bad guys are often the least of your worries. Makes me glad I joined the Navy."

—Dan Bozung
Author of *This Civilian Sh*t Is Hard: From the Cockpit, Cubicle, and Beyond*

"A meticulously detailed account of soldiers in modern war. Ben Warner is a fine example of America's citizen-soldiers, and writes well of carrying the proud tradition of his rich military heritage."

—John Racoosin
Author of *Combat Engineer*

"The military is a world unlike any other. Unless one has spent time in the armed forces, it's impossible to fully appreciate the unique aspects and nuances of military life. Every day can range from mind-numbing boredom to the terror of deadly combat. Only people who carry the burden of carrying out life-and-death assignments on behalf of our country can appreciate what our military does every day. It's an awesome responsibility. Mr. Warner's detailed description of his experiences as a member of one of the first units deployed to Afghanistan following the 9/11 terror attacks allows the rest of us to grasp what life is like for those who fight for America on distant shores. *20-Year Letter* both educates and entertains."

—Bill Murphy
Ex-Marine and Vietnam Veteran, Author of *Not For God and Country*

20-Year Letter
An Afghaninstan Chronicle

By Benjamin R. Warner

© Copyright 2021 Benjamin R. Warner

ISBN 978-1-64663-318-0

Published by

◤ köehlerbooks™

3705 Shore Drive
Virginia Beach, VA 23455
800–435–4811
www.koehlerbooks.com

20-YEAR LETTER

An Afghanistan Chronicle

BENJAMIN R. WARNER

VIRGINIA BEACH
CAPE CHARLES

Dedication

To Porter, Nash Archie, Ellis, and Kora: I hope someday to share these stories, when you are ready. In the event that day doesn't come, here's a record to show why I'm the way I am.

To Betsy: thanks for putting up with someone who constantly burns the candle at both ends. You are my best friend and partner in this crazy life.

CONTENTS

PART I: GETTING THERE

I don't know where I'm going, but I sure know where I've been . . .
—White Snake

THE JOURNEY: STOP ONE

I HAD JUST EXPERIENCED my first flight in the cargo belly of an Airforce C-17 as we touched down in Uzbekistan to drop off a few soldiers from my sister platoon. At that moment, the realness of my situation truly started to hit me. As the cargo door on the tail of the plane began to open, my thoughts were consumed by memories of the last six months of my life and how I came to be here. Our pit stop was scheduled for about thirty minutes—just time enough to load some cargo—and then we were off to Afghanistan, my new home away from home. My mind was racing as I started to piece it all together.

My journey started several months earlier, in March 2002, on a rainy Tuesday. I was working at FedEx at the time and we were on a weather delay due to a late inbound shipment. I chose to take the few hours that I had available to me and head to my reserve unit company headquarters about twenty minutes away to finalize a couple of evaluations. While there, I was approached almost immediately by Frank Mann, a member of the battalion leadership team who ran the day-to-day operations of the unit as a civilian. He proclaimed that he was happy to see me and that he had an urgent question. Our command had received its first mobilization order after 9/11 and one of my sister companies in the battalion had been tasked to complete a mission to go to Fort Lewis, Washington for one year. The duty was primarily to support their ROTC (Reserve Officer's Training Corps) mission as a backfill while one of the units stationed there was deployed overseas. That deploying unit was short one lieutenant on their command team, and he wanted to know if I was interested in filling that slot and deploying with them. Without thinking, I instantly said yes. Honestly, I don't think there is a mission that they would have asked me to complete that I would have turned down in those days. Patriotism was high, and I wanted so badly to serve my country. And just like that, my life would forever change because of the decision that I made that day.

I spent the next few weeks getting my affairs in order and saying my goodbyes, all the while speculating what my future adventures would be. Soon enough, it was time to pack my car and head to Uniontown, Pennsylvania to start the next chapter of my life.

I knew no one in that unit, nor nothing about it walking in the door, so I carried no preconceived notions. I arrived at the unit to not much fanfare and an extremely dysfunctional situation. The unit had a civilian administrator who also served as a full bird colonel (four ranks senior to me) in the Army Reserves. He ran the day-to-day business and pretty much the weekend business, and whatever he said was the law of the land. He would not be deploying, so as I was trying to take over the unit, there was instant friction. Compounding the problem was the fact that he had ruled the unit with an iron fist for so long that none of the leaders had been able to develop. There were some good young soldiers in the unit, but they were being failed by their leadership. As a new lieutenant to the organization, I knew that I would have a mountain of a task on my hands to convince the soldiers to believe in me and to be ready to follow me. Luckily for me, I had a defining moment with the soldiers right away. Ironically this problem almost derailed the mobilization before it started for me and was my first attempt (of many) at career suicide.

This crucial situation arose from something as simple as hotel accommodations for the unit. This may sound trivial, but one of the first lessons that I ever learned in the Army as a leader was to never screw with a soldier's food or living arrangements. One of the civilians who worked at the unit and helped us with administrative tasks had submitted our lodging packet for a local Fairfield Inn, known to be a hotel friendly to business travelers. They had a small gym, pool, and provided breakfast every morning. In his mind, it was everything that we needed. There were two issues I foresaw with this plan: it had no bar (my concern) and was the most expensive option available (taxpayer concern). The lack of a bar may not make sense to some, as we were there for a specific mission to get ready to deploy, but the last thing I needed while we were training was a bunch of drunk soldiers trying to drive back from a bar and getting DUIs. Soldiers like to blow off steam, particularly as they are preparing for their grand send-off. I wanted to make sure there was an option available to them that didn't require driving. I wanted the Holiday Inn; it had a ton of activities included on its grounds (known at the time as a *Holidome*) and met the bar requirement. It was cheaper than the Fairfield Inn, too. But we got neither option. There was a bean counter who saw the request come in and the opportunity to save the taxpayers thousands of dollars on twenty rooms for fifteen nights. He found us a hotel in downtown Uniontown that did not have a brand name, but it did have a bar. In fact, it housed one of the busiest clubs in town. In the beginning, I didn't really think anything of it. I headed to the hotel after the contract was finalized to sign for all the room keys and returned to the reserve center to pass them out. I hadn't been working at my desk more than thirty minutes later when I noticed a line of soldiers at my door. They were in a near-riot situation over the condition of the Uncle Sam-directed rooms. They complained of broken locks, broken windows, blood stains, dirty carpets, and pubic hairs in the bathtubs. I thought that there was no way this could be the truth, so I headed to the hotel myself. It was worse than described. I couldn't help but wonder whether this hotel was reputable or pay-by-the-hour. Sleeping there would have required my government-issued sleeping bag and not taking off my footwear. What I would have given for an iPhone back then to have been able to snap quick photos and send messages instantly. In 2002, I only had a cellular minutes plan and a phone that I could play the snake game on. So, I headed back to the reserve center to raise my complaints.

I started with my company commander, who I had never met and was apparently in the air traveling to Washington state that day as part of our advance party, so he would be no help. My next call was to my battalion headquarters to Mr. Mann, who was the reason I was here in the first place, but he was unavailable. My next call was to my brigade headquarters to the head civilian in charge there, but I could not locate him either. It was a Thursday afternoon and time was critical, so after waiting about five minutes, I escalated my request to my division headquarters. That phone call I was making was the equivalent of the *nuclear option*. I had just steamrolled through three levels of command and was heading to the general officer level. I knew there were some potential ramifications, but I was championing the health and welfare of my soldiers, so I went half-assed full blast. The civilian that I spoke with at that headquarters basically told me that nothing could take place that late in the afternoon. I was directed to release my soldiers to travel home if they wanted to or they could stay at the Fairfield Inn, as it was a previously approved hotel. I was also told that I needed to compile a room-by-room list of all the deficiencies that I saw and to provide a copy to the hotel. They were to have until the following day to correct the items. At this point, I released my soldiers and headed back to the hotel and started making my list. I was using my inner drill sergeant to inspect these rooms, making sure that I found enough stuff that there was no way that they would make us stay there. I finalized my deficiency dissertation, made a copy, and threw my original on the hotel office's desk. I was super proud of my efforts and decided to retire for the evening back to the Fairfield Inn.

I returned to the hotel the following morning and, not surprisingly, nothing had been remedied. At this point, we were relieved from our obligation at this hotel. The civilian I had previously started working with reached back out and we began to work on getting everything reserved for the Holiday Inn. He told me that we had to get the rooms for a certain price or it was a deal-breaker, so I actually did the price negotiation for the government. The hotel manager agreed to my demands, so we ultimately were able to stay at the Holiday Inn. By the following Monday, all had been resolved from a housing standpoint, but I was shown a series of emails that I was not copied on. The first, was a raving recognition that the civilian who originally negotiated the stay had gotten for saving the budgetary day. The second was from that same civilian and included his assessment of the situation. Apparently, he lived in the Uniontown area and had stopped by the controversial hotel over the weekend. He stated that he found nothing wrong with the hotel, but that the command would support my decision. Again, this was a general officer level organization and they were going to let the lowly lieutenant have his way? This was truly his way of saving face. That was the good news of the story. On the opposite end of the spectrum was me. My life over the next few days involved losing several layers of skin from my ass from anyone senior to me (which was a lot of people). I got so many ass-chewings over the phone that over time I began to zone out, to the point where pretty much all I heard resembled the teacher from the old Charlie Brown cartoons: *wah wah, wah wah wah*. The only takeaway that I surmised after it was finally over was that my *bull in a china shop, cowboy* mentality was not appropriate. Officially, I had jumped over several levels of my chain of command and not let anyone help me. Unofficially though, I had been told that I had done the right thing for my soldiers. Either way, I learned a good lesson in those days about what it meant to be right, but maybe not have an appropriate reaction. There was probably a less brash way. In the end, it was all worth it. That hotel situation galvanized a bond with my new soldiers because they knew that I was willing to fight for them. Before long, with all training complete, we were boarding a plane to our next destination—my second stop on this incredible journey.

THE JOURNEY: STOP TWO

WE LEFT FOR FORT LEWIS with a lot of excitement and anticipation but landed with a thud. The day that I volunteered, I signed up for a one year deployment to Fort Lewis in support of Operation Noble Eagle. It was what my country asked me to do. I really hadn't taken the time to actually try to figure out what that would mean. I just wanted to serve my country, even if that meant inside our continental borders. Going to Afghanistan was never part of the initial equation. The anticipation, patriotism and fervor that we all felt as we left Pennsylvania was soon stunted by extreme Army bureaucracy. I honestly cannot think of anything nice to say about my time at Fort Lewis, even nearly twenty years later. To start off, the mission that we were mobilized to complete only needed around thirty soldiers and we arrived with close to 160. One of my sister platoons had the best readiness in the unit so they would get the *honor* of completing that mission. The rest of us were relegated to a life of post chores that involved everything from trash clean-up to grass cutting to weapons range target building. This was in no way what I signed up for and I was angry. We all were. We deployed with an unabashed pride and within weeks, nearly all the winds had left our sails. To compound these issues were the living arrangements. The entire unit, officers, non-commissioned officers, and soldiers alike would stay in World War II-style barracks that had all the comforts you could expect from sixty-year-old, asbestos-filled government housing with poor climate control and communal bathrooms. We were not allowed to bring vehicles and were limited on baggage and comfort items that we could bring. It was basically the equivalent of a bad two-week annual training, but we were supposed to do this for a year.

And just when we thought it couldn't get worse, we met our new command team. The commander of our new Fort Lewis battalion headquarters was pretty young, a high performer who had been promoted early twice (called a *below the zone* promotion). He carried himself with all of this confidence and I instantly felt like we were there to do his bidding for the next year. He could have asked only for the thirty people he needed, but instead he requested an entire organization. That was unfathomable to me.

Worst yet, he was more than happy to parade us around. I remember our "welcome to the new unit" celebration, where he decided to host an officer call for us. This was command-sanctioned drinking and, being in my early twenties, I was all in. The event itself seemed rather harmless, other than being more about our leader than the team he was introducing. I recall that there were a lot of things we discussed and many *good ideas* that he had for us during this drinking marathon that doesn't end until the boss *taps out*. Several hours later, we piled out of this facility and into a van, somewhere between buzzed and hammered. In that moment, this all didn't seem too bad. By the time I awoke the next morning, hazy and with a headache, all had changed. We started receiving multiple calls early on demanding actions on all his suggestions from the night before. I should have known then that this hangover was going to last.

And last it did. From a unit command standpoint, we were treated like second class citizens for the entire time we were stationed there. We carried the stench of being Reservists and we struggled to overcome that, compared to our Active Duty brothers and sisters. It felt as if we could do no right. Now, to be fair, not everyone treated us differently. I served with some fantastic soldiers from our sister Active Duty companies that were supportive of us and tried to help ease our transition, but even with their efforts, it was rough all the while. Captain James Pope, my commander, took the majority of the brunt of seemingly never-ending tirades. He did the best he could not to negatively influence our view of the command, but everyone could see how frequently both he and our entire unit were getting torn down.

I remember when I had first joined the Army, getting mentally prepared for basic training and fully expecting it to be the worst two-plus months of my life. Since I knew my end date as soon as I started, the experience, while mentally taxing, was quite easy for me. I was mentally prepared and that made the actuality of boot camp easier to endure. In contrast, my assumptions of this mobilization could not have been further from reality, and I struggled mightily. As a young lieutenant, it was my job to wear a smile while delegating tasks to my soldiers, which they felt they were getting because they were beneath their Active Duty peers. I completely agreed with them, but I could not flinch and show it. Standing in front of that formation each day absolutely wore me out mentally and emotionally.

Even with all the trials, some benefit did occur for me personally. I started to gain the trust of Captain Pope, my company commander. This was a big deal to me because I was an outsider to the unit, the only officer who was added in before the deployment. The entire command team of officers had been in place well over a year before me. With this newfound trust, I became one his primary sounding boards. While it was great to be someone he could rely upon, it also added a continual burden on me trying to ensure that my team didn't let him down. And we didn't. My platoon was completing all of our assigned tasks to standard and we had also made time to train. We were quickly becoming recognized as the strongest team in the company.

I was really starting to feel pretty good about my team, and I was hoping that the rumblings of a follow-on deployment overseas were true. Yes, we wanted out of Fort Lewis so badly that we were begging for a trip to Afghanistan, which just doesn't seem realistic, but it was. In the summer that year, our battalion received a task to participate in a field training exercise at Yakima Training Center to support a National Guard brigade for their annual training. I was startled to find out that this training center was on the other side of the mountains in Washington State and that it had a desert atmosphere, so we would be able to do some real-world training. As strange as it sounds, I was elated at the possibility of a few weeks in the field doing additional training with my team.

And because nothing ever went smoothly at Fort Lewis, a ripple was soon introduced that further convinced me that our battalion commander wanted my unit to fail. A couple of days before we were supposed to depart, we received word that I would not be training with the company. Instead, I would be a liaison officer between my battalion and unit we were to support. I was infuriated. There were a lot of benefits for me in this from a soldier-comfort standpoint. I wouldn't be required to sleep in the field. I had a barracks room assigned and could shower daily and eat items other than field rations. But none of those comforts meant anything to me. There was a possibility for us to deploy overseas and I wanted to train with my team. How the hell could they do this to me, to us?

With all protests of my new assignment falling on deaf ears, I packed up for the trip to the field and traveled separately from my unit because that's what soldiers do. All in all I must admit that things started really well on this excursion, but not for any reason one would believe. The unit was to convoy to the training site north up I-5 through downtown Seattle and then east to Yakima Training Center on I-90. My commander had been brutalized repeatedly since our arrival for our reporting of our maintenance uptime being far below standard than any other unit in the battalion. However, this convoy proved to be a true measuring stick for my unit. Every vehicle from my unit made the entire convoy of 170 miles with no breakdowns, while my sister units strung vehicles from the front gate of Fort Lewis all the way to Yakima. Multiple vehicles broke down in downtime Seattle in particular, which made what was already a terrible city traffic situation, much worse. This four-hour movement turned into a fourteen-hour ordeal. All the while I had to feign that I cared about the plight of the other units, when deep down I struggled to contain my smile. Unfortunately for my battalion commander, the return home trip was worse. This gave my commander a couple-week reprieve from the brow beatings he normally received but served more as a stay of execution over a technicality that we knew was still coming.

As far as my time as a liaison officer, it was terrible. It was mostly made up of eighteen-hour plus workdays where I commuted from location to location in the field, all under blackout driving conditions. So, while my stops may not have been far apart, our five miles-per-hour speed made them feel like they were. The only saving grace that I had was an assigned driver. We kept each other going, as he would drop me off at meetings and sleep while I was inside, and I would sleep while he was driving me from place to place. I was so tired that many nights, when I did find my bed, I would simply remove my boots and fall over without taking off another article of clothing. I was pissed at the job that was given to me, but there was no way I was going to fail at it. In the end, I was recognized for performing my duties well, but it was just frustrating to me that I barely saw my soldiers and I felt like I lost valuable time with them.

Once we returned from the field, the rumors of our overseas deployment started to hit a fever pitch, so they started lessening some of our requirements for base tasks in order to let us train more often. In subsequent years there was training guidance and a lot of boxes to check before one could deploy, but in this situation, we were basically flying blind. We had some basic soldier tasks that we needed to be good at, as well as having soldiers that were technically competent. That was pretty much it. Our guidelines were our basic instincts and feelings. I seriously miss those days.

Soon, we were instructed to also start taking block leave to allow soldiers time at home before heading overseas. We still didn't have a date yet, but we went ahead and split the unit in two and started sending people home. I had been told unofficially that my platoon would be leading the Afghanistan mission and I was sent home with the first group in order to get back to Fort Lewis to make final mission preparations. At the time, I wasn't married, nor did I have any kids, so this trip in my mind was set to be a final, memorable blowout. I tried really hard to make that so and for all intents and purposes it was for all those around me. For me personally though, everything was completely overshadowed by what I knew was coming. It was next to impossible not to be consumed by it. I was twenty-three years old and I was going to lead a group of men and women to war—the greatest unknown any of us would ever experience. And to make matters worse, I couldn't tell anyone!

I enjoyed my time at home, but not as much as I could have. I was preoccupied with the coming deployment and counting down the time to go back and do the damned thing. This was very selfish of me. First of all, I wasn't truly there for my loved ones. And then several of my soldiers didn't get the same opportunity to spend time with their families that I had been given but didn't take full advantage of. We finally got our alert halfway into the second wave of leave. Once our deployment order was published, we had to call everyone back immediately. It was our time to go.

Communicating with everyone at home on leave would be really easy today, but at that time there was no social media and most of my soldiers didn't have cell phones. We were calling landlines. In most situations, I was able to talk to the soldiers directly, but there were a few where I got to be the person to tell a mother that their child was going to war and I needed them back ASAP. I could seriously feel what it meant to basically paralyze someone over the phone. I know that I said over and over again to all that everything was going to be okay, but those were hollow promises. I had no idea what the hell was going to happen.

A few days later, everyone had returned and we were packing up for the scariest thing that any of us had ever done. All that we knew was that we were going to make everyone proud.

AFGHANISTAN BOUND

WITH EVERYONE BACK in the unit, we started our countdown. I don't know the words to accurately describe the day you are going to deploy or the days leading up to it, as it's basically a roller coaster of every emotion one can seriously feel. Everyone has counted down to birthdays or Christmas or the last day of school, but this was a more ominous date. I wanted out of Fort Lewis so badly that I would have done anything to leave it, but as we got closer and closer to the date to fly, the gravity started to set in. I have done the deployment countdown three times now, but nothing equaled this first time, as I didn't know which way was up or down and I felt like I was equal parts terrified and excited. I was selected to fly out on our advance party and would lead the first team hitting boots on the ground in Afghanistan. I was happy for this honor, but it only compounded my emotions, as the challenge of just trying to get to Afghanistan was tough. Our journey was like acting out a play with a script only half-written. The mission was to get to Afghanistan, but the path included a commercial flight from Seattle to Baltimore, then catching what we called the *Freedom Bird* from Baltimore to Germany, with a final destination of Turkey, where we would have to coordinate our own way into Afghanistan. The irony of the plane that was going to take me to war being called the Freedom Bird was not lost on me, as with every stop on this voyage, we had fewer freedoms than the one before it.

Since we were traveling as a small team instead of a full unit, the task of trying to travel with weapons proved to be our biggest stumbling block. It was critical that we had our weapons when our feet hit the ground in Afghanistan, but there was no easy way to get them there. In order to travel out of Seattle, we were told that we needed to have a weapons box built at Fort Lewis that would carry all our M-16s. Like all good soldiers, we did as we were told, but the final product that was delivered to the unit was the equivalent of sailing with a boat anchor dragging. It was sturdy, bulky, and exceptionally heavy. With the omission of size and weight, the origins of this box were quite benign, but they became a pain in my ass quickly. We arrived at the Seattle airport and everything went as planned, as the first leg had been well-coordinated. As the OIC (officer in charge), I was designated to escort the weapons until they made it to the secure area, and I was able to check this box easily. Everything that happened after this flight with these weapons was much more difficult to execute.

I must have been completely clueless to the weapons scenario, as extraordinary care was given to getting them into a secure area in Seattle, but I wasn't given any further instructions about picking them up in Baltimore. I had to personally walk this box of weapons of war into a secure area, but once we arrived at Baltimore Washington Airport (BWI), I reacquired the box at baggage claim. No ID was required, just grab it and go. I'm not saying this was a security risk though, as it would have taken an Olympic body builder to grab this box and get away quickly.

We were not transferring flights at BWI, as our next plane was scheduled for the following day, so we were literally picking up our crate of weapons and playing guard duty for the night. I am fairly confident that this would never happen today. I felt like this overnight at a government rate-friendly hotel in an unpleasant neighborhood was the equivalent of birds taking turns sitting on a nest. That's about how dangerous we were, as we had no weapons or ammo with which to guard the weapons we were trying to protect. Making matters more frustrating was the fact that we all got to spend our final night in the States babysitting a bunch of weapons that we couldn't leave. As the person in charge I could have easily just assigned others to watch the weapons and had one final hurrah stateside, but that just didn't seem right. Everyone staying at that hotel was a trusted member of the unit and had each previously displayed the traits of being servant leaders, that's why they were selected to go on the advance party in the first place. That night was no different. Misery loved company, as we spent the evening together, growing more nervous about where we were going.

After an uneventful night, we arrived at the airport for the next phase of our trip and we had a hurdle immediately introduced. Our tank of a weapons box was identified as too large and could not get on the plane with us. Although I was extremely angry about this, I only protested a little because it would have wasted time, and we needed to act quickly. We were still able to secure our weapons, they just needed to be in smaller containers. And securing the weapons was a big deal to me because I had flashbacks of traveling to Egypt the previous year for the Army. In that scenario, I flew out of a secure military installation (Pope Air Force Base) and into a military base in Germany. We had to take the bolts out of our weapons, preventing them from being able to fire, and carry them in our cargo pockets. The weapons were placed at our feet, which was especially uncomfortable. Adding to the madness of securing these weapons, we had to leave two soldiers on the airplane per cabin during refueling to guard the rifles that had no capability of being fired in the middle of a secure military installation. To this day, I still can't think of a good reason why we had to go through all of that. It all just seemed a bit overboard. With that previous experience in mind, we tried to adapt quickly, as our supply sergeants ran out and bought us new foot lockers. I remember asking an airline employee if we could go to a private area to transfer weapons and was shocked that I was told no. So I found myself in the BWI airport on the one-year anniversary of 9/11, in the middle of the passenger ticketing area, wearing civilian clothes, and cracking into our box of weapons to hand them out to transfer them. We must have looked like we were trying to assault the airport. Security had been notified of what we were doing, but I know there was an uneasy feeling among the other passengers. I didn't hear anyone scream or see anyone run, but people were trying to quickly get away from us. Our excitement only lasted a few minutes, and before long we had everything checked in and we were heading to security. I felt like this was one of the slow walks that you see in the movies where the day is about to get saved (think *Armageddon*), but the reality was that Fort Lewis was now behind us and all we wanted to do was get to the sandy place. From here, our goals were simple: make our friends and family proud, serve our country, and, most importantly, stay alive.

Our flight was relatively peaceful to Germany, and after a short refueling period, we were off again and headed to Turkey. This was the spot where the civilian clothes would go away and we would actually start carrying our weapons. Once we arrived, it was surprisingly easy to get our next flight coordinated, and we broke for the evening knowing that the next day would begin our wild adventure. I made one last phone call home and spent most of the night staring at the ceiling of the large communal tent dosing off and on. I thought about family, I thought about friends, and I thought about mission. There were probably thirty people sleeping around me, but it was probably the most alone I have ever felt.

THE DARKNESS

THERE WASN'T MUCH EXCITEMENT the next morning, and before long, we were all staged at the airfield, ready to depart. Once we boarded, we knew we would be stopping once in Uzbekistan to drop off a few members of our unit and to take care of some logistics items, and then we would be on our way. All I truly remember from our first stop was that it was sparse, which I predicted, but also much cooler than I expected. It was also, conveniently for them, still daylight. Our arrival to our new normal would be a night landing, which at that time meant nothing to me.

Looking back now, I had no idea how miscalculated that opinion was, as the darkness there was a whole other level than anything I had ever previously experienced. Growing up in Charleston, West Virginia, I got the experience of living near a city, but was never more than twenty minutes away from a rural area. I bring this up because, without the ambient glow of city lights, it can get very dark where I grew up, except for maybe the distant glow of some summertime fireflies. Or at least, that's what I thought was dark. I was mistaken. As I took this roundabout path to get to Afghanistan (I'm pretty sure there's not a direct path), at twenty-three years old, I found myself trying to catch a nap on an aircraft skid of cargo on the last leg of this journey. Being September 2002, the US had only been in country with boots on the ground a few months, so there wasn't exactly a playbook on what was to come. I knew we were getting close, as I found myself staring anxiously at the roof of the plane when the pilot made the announcement that it was time to land. I scurried back to my seat and strapped myself in, and immediately I felt the plane start to plunge. It turns out that all airfield landings in those days were combat landings for security reasons. That meant that the plane would approach the airfield still at a high elevation and basically act like a corkscrew, spinning around and down, until finally landing. I also found out some time later that all cargo planes would shoot off flares as they were landing to divert any heat seeking devices that could be fired at us. At the time, I didn't know the reason behind any of this. All I knew was that we were quickly plummeting from a high altitude, my stomach was in my throat, and my ears were screaming from the drop in altitude. Finally, we landed with a sigh of relief and, luckily, clean underwear. This was all quickly replaced with a little bit of nervous anxiety and a whole lot of fear. Being the only officer on the plane-turned-roller coaster during landing, I was told I would lead the group off of the aircraft.

I moved to the rear of the plane and waited for the cargo door to open. As the door slowly lowered, my first memory was of a blowing dry heat hitting my face and then what seemed to be an endless sea of darkness. I was handed a chem light, which is the military version of a glow stick, and told to move out. It was then mentioned in passing to be careful not to step off the runway because the area had not been cleared of land mines. My heart sank almost instantly. I felt petrified. Everything around me was black, a darkness that I can only compare to walking around with your eyes closed. I could stretch my arms out in front of me and could only make out the silhouette of my hands. All I could think was *Holy shit. I'm going to step off this runway and get my leg blown off because all I have to guide me is some damned glowing green liquid.* I must have looked like a cross between the

Quasimodo and a penguin waddling across the tundra while on my shuffle. I had my rucksack on and I hunched over as I moved, my feet sliding forward as I tried not to die. After the longest hundred-yard-waddle of my life, I had successfully traversed my way to a reception tent where we got our country in brief and were told to find our stuff at a collection point, where about a foot of loose sand had piled up. I sifted through the sand trying to find my belongings, all the while still thinking about land mines in the back of my head.

I was able to get settled in that first night, and I started to get my bearings during the next few days. I began to feel better and more aware of my surroundings, and even had a hint of confidence, which quickly disappeared when the darkness would creep up on me again. We had begun our pursuit of assuming control of the ammunition supply point (ASP), which happened to be situated on the back side of the base. We were also in charge of its guard force. The first night that my soldiers were on duty, I chose to go visit them. Due to the infant stage of our operations, we were practicing light discipline, even on the interior of the base, so I had to drive without head lights, which we called *blackout*, while wearing night vision goggles (NVGs). I had never driven with NVGs previously, but foolishly chose not to ask for help. It appears my confidence had gotten the best of me. In my mind, all I could think was *how hard could it be*? I was too proud to admit that I didn't know what I was doing. With today's night vision, this drive would have been a breeze, but the generation PV5 goggles that I had were less sophisticated than some of the toys kids have these days. Most of the drive path wasn't paved or graveled, but was loose sand, and the only thing guiding my driving were strands of concertina wire strung along the sides of the route. The purpose of this wire was to keep you from driving into a mine field. Once I got off the hard road in the middle of the base and onto the sand, I knew instantly that I had made a potentially grave mistake. I only had about two miles to travel, and even while driving with all the caution in the world, I still couldn't see a damned thing. It wasn't long before I misjudged a curve and buried the HUMVE in the wire. The swearing that I did when I realized what had happened was replaced with relief that the wire had potentially saved my life, or at least a few limbs.

The next several minutes were some of the longest and most stressful of my life, as I tried to free the vehicle from the jagged wire on the edge of what felt like nowhere. With a lot of luck and a good deal of sweat, I was able to free the HUMVE without slashing my hands, which was a minor miracle since I had no gloves. I was able to navigate my way the rest of the way to the ASP and complete my mission that night. I immediately escalated my incident to our command and they were able to compel the departing unit to leave their night vision devices behind. My first drive with better technology was a night and day difference—pun intended. Over the course of the eight months I spent in country, I never experienced any additional issues caused by the nighttime darkness, but I certainly respected it. For anyone that ever wants to experience it, all you have to do is close your eyes.

The darkness was the first of many things that I had acclimate myself to. It was certainly not the last, as I got acquainted with my new life on deployment.

PART II: THE LIFE

This learning to live again is killing me . . .
—Garth Brooks

THE REAL WORLD: AFGHANISTAN EDITION

IN THE EARLY 1990S, the new phenomenon of reality TV swept through MTV, in the days when it actually played music videos. The show was called *The Real World*, and it profiled the lives of seven strangers who entered a house voluntarily and agreed to be filmed. The gold of the show was what would happen when everyone lost their filters. I like to think of my time in Afghanistan through the same lens but without the amazing house—or alcohol, for that matter. In fact, my eight tentmates and I could have fit in one bedroom of that house. We were there voluntarily, for the most part, but there were no cameras. Things got *real*, and quick.

There are a lot of challenges one faces when deployed but getting used to the living conditions is one of the worst. Boot camp in each service begins in a lot of ways by introducing everyone to communal living, where you find out that you are no longer in charge of your own comforts. This was reinforced during several trips to the field to train since I had enlisted. In each of these excursions, I learned and refined my skills to make life better, and a goal I had each day was to improve my own personal *foxhole*. But even the trips to the field were short in nature, and I basically just started an hour-by-hour countdown until I could go home as soon as I began unpacking.

Nothing that I had done had truly gotten me ready to deployed living conditions, particularly at the beginning of this operation. Once conflicts get more mature, living accommodations are much better, but in the beginning, it is just rough. When my forty-five soldiers and I arrived in Afghanistan, I think it brought the base population up to about 900, and there was housing available for about 850. There was no temporary housing available for transients, so we had to pack into the same tents that the unit we were replacing had spread out in over the previous several months. To say we were crammed in like sardines would have been an understatement. My first night was pretty much a blur once we made it to our tents, but I was pleasantly surprised to see an air conditioner mounted at the end of my tent when I woke up the next morning. It turns out that each of the tents we were falling in on had air conditioning, and I thought, at least for a few moments, that it would make it better. That was until I discovered that the unit was powering their tents off one generator and that there wasn't enough power available to run all seven air conditioners (one in each tent) at once. Apparently, there was only enough electric power to run the cooling units in two tents at a time before breakers started tripping. The seven tents played *musical air conditioning* all day. It was better than nothing, but at the same time terribly frustrating.

This living arrangement would be a temporary condition, as new tents were being built that would include some form of climate control. There was some hope on the horizon. We just needed to wait a short period of time and they would be ready to go. They were to be larger than what we were currently staying in, and we were told that the standard would be nine to ten soldiers per tent. As construction began, there was one thing that I found particularly peculiar about the tents. They were built off the ground, which we were told was due to the rainy season. I can't imagine how dumb the look on my face was when I was told this. I just kept thinking, *Rainy season in the desert? I'll believe it when I see it*. Regardless, I was just happy to know that climate control was coming. I had come to accept the fact that I was going to be sleeping on a cot for the next several months and that I would no longer have any personal space.

The showers and laundry were the next large barrier with which I had to get accustomed. The Army has entire military units that are dedicated to providing field laundry and bath services, but I learned pretty much instantly that apparently those are just for show when you do training exercises. Once we occupy a country, it's nearly always the first thing to be outsourced to a local vendor, so the chances of finding someone that speaks a common language to air any complaints wasn't a realistic expectation. As far as showering is concerned, there are some soldiers that feel that going without showers is a badge of honor. I am pro-shower and therefore not a member of that team, nor honestly do I understand why anyone would choose that if a shower is available. To quote one of my military mentors, Tom Cannington, "You don't have to live hard to be hard." Now that my *you should take shower* soap box moment is over, I will admit that there were many days that I did not participate in this ritual cleaning activity. Whether the water was so hot that it would have removed layers of skin, or so cold that it would take hours to recover in the winter, it was rarely a fully satisfying experience. The unpredictable water temperatures were a pain, but most days it was coupled with a perpetually stopped-up shower drain. This led to taking showers in ankle-deep, filthy water. I tried to ignore it, but there was always a thought in the back of my mind about the nastiness that I was standing in. Add that to the fact that my tent city didn't have a whole lot of gravel to weigh down the blowing sand, so it was not uncommon to return from the shower on a breezy day dirtier than when I started. Any way I looked at it, being dirty was my new standard.

The laundry situation wasn't much better. First off, the laundry contractor didn't use detergent to clean the clothing because of disposal concerns. Instead, they just used exceptionally hot water.

This would wash off any visible exterior dirt but didn't do much for deep cleaning. Over time, the back collars of the uniforms started to develop grease-like stains from the excess sweat coming off our necks. By the time this occurred, I had already become numb to the filthy conditions, so it wasn't something that I much noticed. But it would become a source of pain for me later.

The second biggest issue with the laundry contractor was the aforementioned language barrier of its employees. We had to inscribe a special code that was unique to each us on all of our clothing. We turned in laundry twice a week and I am fairly certain that the exception was getting all of your items back correctly. Outside of uniform tops, I know that pretty much everything else I turned in ended up in one big base clothing swap. This wasn't the end of the world to me, as it related to t-shirts and socks, but was damn near depressing when I received someone else's underwear. I had gotten used to the filth and the dirt but wearing another man's underwear was not a bridge I was ready to cross.

The last of the creature comforts to get used to from a living standpoint had to be the portalets. I am fairly certain that before I joined the Army that I had never had to shit in a portalet, but as I arrived on this base, I knew that this would become ritual. Never in a million years of my life did I think that I would be writing a story about *blue palaces*, but they were an additional part of my frustration. To start off, there weren't enough of them. Worse, they were a long walk from my tent so any need in the middle of the night or first thing in the morning required a hike. The distance may have only been a few hundred feet, but it could feel like a mile.

Back to the fact that there weren't enough portalets, though. I basically had to train my body what times of day it could use the restroom. First thing in the morning was a *no-go,* as they were usually filled to nearly the seat, a visual I still have seared in my mind. Right after daily cleaning wasn't an option either, because the cleaners left so much extra chemical in the poop thrones that the splash back made everyone look like they had sat on a Smurf and it had subsequently exploded.

Compounding the sanitary conditions in the portalets were the large number of local nationals that worked on base each day. They believed that sitting on toilet seats was dirty (in retrospect, they may have been onto something), so they stood on the seats to do their business. After a short period of time, the mud, dirt, and constant fear of contracting tuberculosis for all service members forced us to designate separate facilities for them. This, in turn, took more facilities away from the total population.

And just when I thought that the restroom facility issue couldn't get any worse, summer hit and I learned a hard lesson in life that I carry to this day: breaking a sweat while taking a poop may quite possibly be one of the grossest feelings in the world. By then though, gross had become customary.

And then, the grand finale of poor living conditions arrived with the aforementioned rainy season. I didn't understand why they built the tents off the ground and then it started raining. Before long I felt like it had rained for forty days and forty nights nonstop, and I was fairly certain that Noah was going to come sailing by at any moment with his boat full of livestock. The country had horrible natural drainage and there was pooling water outside of our tents. This lead to three problems: trouncing through ankle deep water to go pee, starting each day with wet boots just getting out of the tent, and my favorite, the need to take antimalarial medicine due to the subsequent infestation of mosquitos. The military's drug of choice to combat this problem was Mefloquine, and we affectionately called our weekly ritual of taking the pills *Mefloquine Monday's* because we had to stand in formation to hand out the pills and make sure everyone took them. This began as an evening ritual, but before long the drug's side effects of anxiety and hallucinations really started to affect soldiers in their sleep, and we had to change our consumption proceeding to first thing in the morning. I once had a graphic dream where I was shot multiple times. It felt so real and unnerved me to the point of waking up in a puddle of sweat. Once we started taking the pills in the morning, I had no further issues, but that dream was enough to last me a lifetime.

BLACK BETTY

THERE WAS ANOTHER RIPPLE in the Mefloquine conundrum, which was the fact that we were heavily armed. Our magazines were loaded in our weapons, and everyone had at least 210 rounds in their possession. In my subsequent deployments, we carried ammunition magazines with us, but not loaded. Each time we would have a meal or at nearly all structures we entered, we would have to use a clearing barrel, to verify that our weapons were safe. Afghanistan was much different. The only time that the magazines left our weapons was when we cleaned them. This exasperated the issues with the drug's side effects. The last thing we needed was a soldier waking up in the middle of the night having drug-induced hallucinations and start shooting people. As mentioned previously though, our schedule to take the medicine changed to accommodate this, but I still had to wonder how the risk assessment had been conducted on the malaria medicine in the first place.

All of that being said, just carrying a weapon, in general, was another pain in the ass to get used to. Don't get me wrong, I wanted to have protection available, but there was just no comfortable way to carry a rifle around base every moment of the day or night. A pistol could be put in a holster and at times forgotten that it was there. A rifle, on the other hand, was clunky and cumbersome. They were also a little dangerous. One quick move from you or your battle buddy and you could really knock the shit out of someone or yourself. My weapon was tethered to my side continually. I took it to the portalet with me and tucked it in to a safe spot each night when I went to bed. It accompanied me to watch movies and make phone calls. The only times it wasn't within my arm's reach was when I showered, walked the ASP at work, and when I ran the path on base. In those situations, someone had to safeguard it for me. The running part was the worst, but I will get to that later.

Soldiers both fawned over and resented those that carried pistols because the only time that anyone wanted a rifle by their side was when they went off base. Carrying a 9mm pistol was nice and all when you were in a secure base environment, but as soon as you left the wire, no one wanted anything to do with a pistol. Afghanistan had an opioid and hash problem and the last thing anyone desired was to be confronted by someone who was so high that they were out of their mind and be carrying a weapon that couldn't knock them down. At the time, we still carried the M-16s, which were long-barreled, so from a close-quarter standpoint, there was a risk. This was still viewed as a better option than a pistol outside the wire, though, which posed the same threat whether you threw it at or fired it at someone.

I titled this chapter *Black Betty* because every rifle, like all trucks, need to have a name. Most men choose a woman's name. I don't know if naming your steel companion was a sick way to try to make life comfortable or just the affection that you grow toward your weapon. Either way, it was the most important thing that we had in our possession. We cared for it daily because we knew two truths: we would never leave her and she would never leave us, and we wanted to make damn sure she fired when we pulled the trigger. She couldn't let us down.

I can honestly say that as time passed, I never really got that comfortable carrying Betty around, but she did become an extension of me. Believe it or not, I missed her dearly when I got home. Okay, well, not intentionally. During my first true celebration after getting home and after consuming far too many adult beverages, I declared that I could not leave the bar until I found my rifle. I'm sure my drunk ass was a sight to see that night. To make matters more embarrassing (then and now) was the fact that as I was freaking out that I lost my weapon, I also got confused about my sleeping arrangements. My sister had booked a room for the night at the Embassy Suites, but I declared that I was at the wrong embassy when a friend attempted to drop me off. I was adamant that I needed to go to the US Embassy in Kabul. Apparently, my stubborn self needed some convincing. Needless to say, I slept well that night.

GENERAL ORDER NUMBER 1

FROM THE END of the previous story, it is pretty easy to infer that I was a lightweight when it came to drinking by the time I arrived home. That's because I had been sober for the last several months. You see, the Army has rules of conduct for everything that we do. Included in this is the Uniform Code of Military Justice, which lays out all the extra things we can get in trouble for that are not technically violations of any other laws. For our deployments overseas, we added in another wrinkle, General Order Number 1. This order provided multiple prohibitions, including disturbing or destroying historic artifacts, entering mosques for non-Muslim personnel, photography restrictions, and possession of privately owned firearms. These additional rules all seemed to pretty much be common sense, but the order did carry with it a few other prohibitions that would have an impact. These restrictions involved gambling, alcohol, and pornography. I mention gambling more as a concern over idle time and the propensity of soldiers for playing cards. The formula of cards, boredom, and growing bank accounts could make soldiers take stupid monetary risks, so it was a point that we drove home to our soldiers frequently, but one that we didn't spend a lot of time enforcing. As long as no one complained, no one was getting punished.

Now the prohibition of alcohol and pornography was an entirely different story. Restricting a soldier's access to both goes against just about everything that is standard about the Army. Each and every military base that has a permanent force stationed there has six consistent structures: a post exchange (or PX, the military's version of Walmart or Target), grocery store, gas station, fast food place, donut shop, and a class VI store. The military definition of class VI is *personal demand items*, but the primary purpose of all military class VI stores is alcohol sales. Drinking is a heavy part of the culture in the armed forces, and one of the primary factors that allows for it, in my opinion, is physical training (PT). At my civilian job now, a deterrent to spending all night drinking is that my job would be in jeopardy if I showed up in the early morning still feeling the effects of last night and smelling of it. The Army has a built-in detox program at the start of every day. No one really pays attention to the shape anyone is in as they stand in formation in the early morning. After an hour of physical activity and possibly some vomiting, with a quick shower, we are all ready to tackle the day. The fact that we are then not agonizing through the recovery begets the ability to feel like we can do it again. It's a perpetual cycle. Couple this with the age of most junior soldiers and it's very easy to see where this could lead.

At times, drinking is also encouraged and rewarded by higher commands. I briefly described a story earlier about sanctioned drinking during an officer call at the beginning of my time at Fort Lewis, but that wasn't the last time that alcohol played a role while I was there. One of the first weekends that we were assigned to Fort Lewis, we had been dismissed on a Friday with no weekend training planned. I was fully anticipating the ability to blow off some steam until about an hour after our workday ended, when I got a call from my battalion headquarters. My excitement was expeditiously crushed as the voice on the other end of the line informed me that there was a scheduling error for weekend duty and that I was being designated as the on-call officer for the weekend. I swore under my breath but then agreed to return to duty. With this, all weekend plans were shot, as I had to be within a short commute of the headquarters and no drinking was allowed. As I stewed with disdain about the trap that I had fallen into, I began to devise ways to ensure that this would never happen to me again. It didn't take long for me to develop an irrational solution. I would start drinking at the end of each Friday workday and if called, I would be too drunk to work. As ridiculous as this plan was, I executed the following weekend and the one after and it did remedy my problem. I received the same phone call on the second weekend, but this time, I had already started drinking so they went to the next person on the list. Problem solved. Strangely, I continued this activity going forward for all the weekends that we didn't have something scheduled, but I never received another scheduling error call again.

Back to Afghanistan. I had no concerns over my ability to stay away from alcohol but was worried about my soldiers. My only saving grace was that alcohol was not readily available in country, so soldiers had to work hard to get it, which certainly helped limit a lot of the potential problems. Flare-ups did occur, as most of our coalition partners were not held to the same regulations as us. I vividly remember the Italian Army dropping off some meat, cheese, and wine at my tent the night before I was to leave to have a celebration of our time in country and friendships we had built. The look on my face had to have been excruciating as I barked at them to get the wine out of the tent as quickly as possible. It was too close to the end to make that mistake publicly. All this said, we didn't have a single negative report in my unit for drinking. That's not to say no one did it, just more of the fact that it was well-policed and as a young lieutenant, I appreciated that.

The same way that a military base has six standard businesses inside the base perimeter, there are three pillar businesses that usually operate within a one-block radius outside a base. These are pawn shops, tattoo parlors, and strip clubs. For the tattoo piece, no one was in a huge hurry to get a tattoo in Afghanistan. For sanitary reasons, this may have been the most common-sense decision available. I am sure many were planning their new tattoos for when they got home and as the deployment progressed, the size of their desired ink grew larger and larger—at least I knew these were sober thoughts.

The pawn shops gave soldiers quick access to cash, which then allowed them to participate in some other vice, usually drinking, tattoos, and the strip clubs. The strip clubs around bases made money, more on the weekends that soldiers got paid, less on the other weekends when service members were cash strapped, but they were always well-supported. The military has the perfect demographic to support these establishments, generally young, male, unmarried, and with disposable income available. Uncle Sam gives his soldiers access to three hot meals a day and a place to sleep. With basic needs met, nearly everything a soldier makes is disposable.

Although this environment was familiar to soldiers, base life in Afghanistan was much different. To be culturally sensitive, we banned pornography of any kind in Afghanistan as part of General Order Number 1 as well. The irony behind this was pretty funny though, as I had multiple conversations about pornography with the locals. One that always comes to mind was an Afghani businessman who did some contract work on the base, including construction services (pre-fab buildings and other structures). He loved to visit my work site, where he could always be counted on to steal peanuts (once he put his hand in the can, we just gave it to him due to tuberculosis concerns). I also don't think he ever came to the site when he didn't ask if I had any magazines with the *big sexy women*. He declared himself a devout Muslim but wanted to be clear that he would take any smut I would give him. I casually declined each time, as I never had any in my possession. In another example, we had the merchants that sold bootleg movies on the base who constantly would ask if we wanted any pornographic movies. Again, I declined each time, but did hear rumor that they could get their hands on anything that one may desire, which was pretty concerning given the environment.

THE LOCALS

SPEAKING OF THE LOCALS, Afghanistan as a country resembled a place where time had been standing still for decades. For anyone that doesn't understand the toll of war on a land or the rise and rule of a terroristic organization like the Taliban, they need to look no further than Afghanistan to see the devastation and poverty that it caused. The locals that I met were humble, proud, and worked hard. But they were also poor and hungry. The first word that I learned in Farsi, their national tongue, was *baksheesh*, or "give." The children were constantly asking for us to give them items. For the most part we obliged as much as possible, usually with leftover rations from our meals. There were specific humanitarian missions to provide for the villagers, but for us, there was nothing formal to offer to the community. Anything we gave away was thrown from a moving vehicle, as it was too dangerous to stop. We had to be very careful doing this though, as it was also exceptionally dangerous; not for us, but for the children who would receive our offerings. They had no fear of anything, and if I threw candy or a ration packet out of the back of a truck, they would not hesitate to run between vehicles to be the first to get it. We set a policy in my unit that only the last vehicle would provide items for the kids because we almost endured multiple accidents trying to avoid striking a child.

Even with the extreme poverty, some people in the country were very well-to-do. I dealt with a lot of truck drivers whose vehicles were so dated that they had to start them by hand-crank. I had never witnessed anything like this before, as this equipment was several generations old. These dated trucks were juxtaposed by brand new SUVs and Mercedes-Benzes. These belonged to the local warlords, who acted as regional governors throughout the country. These rulers maintained control of their respective areas and set up contracts that were designed to stimulate the economy, all the while lining their own pockets. They got a cut of everything, including a portion of the pay that locals received for working on base each day. The justification for this was a paid income tax, but this money went toward no improvement projects or infrastructure. The only thing paying this burden provided was the ability to continue to work.

And work they did. Hundreds of local nationals would line up each day at the entry-control point of our base. There were several set projects that several locals would be tasked for each day, but our unit could also request support for projects each day. The only requirements that we had to provide to receive laborers were an armed soldier escort for each group of ten local nationals each and a spare portalet. The spare portalet wasn't a specific requirement but would simply become a necessity as soon as workers were brought to your area. With the constant fear of tuberculosis and the associated concern of skin-to-skin contact with the locals, one would soon be down a rest facility after work began.

At the end of each week, the locals that worked on base would be paid in cash, somewhere around five dollars a week. As they would walk out our gates, they would proceed straight to pay their required taxes to their warlord. While this was frustrating to see, one has to understand that the currency of Afghanistan was basically defunct. It was still utilized but the exchange rate was something crazy like 1500 to one from Afghani to American. This money was a form of a living wage for the people, as small as it seemed to me.

Income inequality was a real thing in that country with no middle
class. Power was wielded monetarily. The flood of American dollars
that bombarded the country did find its way to some of the average
Afghani, but a larger percentage found its way into the pockets of
the regional rulers. Most of the business owners just scraped by.
One of the most telling moments of my time there involved a trip
to a computer supply shop in Kabul. We were buying printers, ink
cartridges, and various other ancillary computer accessories for use
on the base. These were items that we could generally get through
the Army supply system, but due to long lead times, we chose to
procure them locally, which provided an added benefit to provide
cash to spur their economy. As I entered the shop, I noted that they
did sell computers, but ironically, they didn't use any computers to
run their business. We were given a hand-written paper receipt and
the shop owner used a cash box to collect our money. The oddity
of buying computer parts from a computer store that didn't utilize
computers was not lost on me, but it was a further indication of the
locals in that country just trying to get by.

THE PX AND THE RISE OF DHL

WE WERE ALL JUST TRYING to get by. I did a lot of harping previously about the lack of comforts overseas, and this will be my opportunity to continue beating that dead horse because purchasing anything overseas that I needed was a massive challenge. If I run out of something at home, I can run out to the store and buy it. Plus, thanks to Amazon, I can usually have just about anything delivered to my door within twenty-four hours, not to mention all of the store locations around me that are open around the clock. In Afghanistan there weren't a whole lot of buying options. Anything that I wanted or needed had to be able to fit in a box that the post office could ship, and it also had to be capable of clearing a customs declaration. Getting someone to ship something to me was only half the battle because the item then had to make it halfway around the world intact. And transportation was the biggest shortfall of all. As time would drag on, Bagram Airfield would become the crown jewel of deployment locations in Afghanistan, but in 2002, it more closely resembled a lump of coal. Being bordered by Iran to the west and south and Pakistan to the east, the only option for freight movement over land was to bring deliveries in from the north, but due to the significant Taliban strong holds in the mountains, this was not considered as an option. This effectively meant that anything that needed to get into the country had to be flown in. Items to support the mission took priority for all air transport, as they should, so there wasn't much left over to provide for soldiers' luxuries.

As young soldiers, we are brained washed right away about the post exchange (PX) and all of its greatness. In basic training, it was a sweet reprieve to get to go purchase toiletries while supervised because at least I could control what I bought. The situation at the PX in Afghanistan in contrast, continued to hammer home the point that there was nothing comfortable about war. I guess I should have been happy that they had a PX and I probably would have been, had I not waited in an exceptionally long line outside of this converted bombed-out building (the gravity of which wasn't lost on me), just to take a look at what was inside. Any excitement that I felt before I walked in was quickly extinguished once I surveyed the store where the most comforting items that I could find were spicy peanuts, dancing James Brown dolls (like how the hell did this end up here?), and sardines in soybean oil. They also had a robust greeting card section for any holiday that wasn't relevant to the moment, like Mother's Day cards in September, all the Hallmark leftovers from the powerhouse celebrations of Boss's Day, Administrative Professionals' Day, and hell, maybe even Bring-Your-Dog-to-Work Day. As obligated as I felt to buy something after waiting in a long line, I just couldn't bring myself to pull that trigger. I guess I should have been happy that there were some options for me, as a short time into my deployment I took a trip to Kandahar to one of the southern military bases to check on some logistics issues. While there, I discovered that their PX had succumbed to an electrical fire about a week before I got there and their service members had nothing. They just started rebuilding because it is what we did.

The PX situation did get much better as time progressed and before I left country, they had opened a new facility, this time in a renovated, bombed-out building. This *upscale* renovation only included air conditioning, lighting, and paint, but it did make it feel less like a condemned structure that was about to collapse. Before it got better though, it did provide one more display of cruel irony. The pickings inside the building as mentioned were quite slim, and there were always promises of it getting better. They started making announcements that we had a container of soda that was going to be flown in (yes this was big news) and that caused a fever-pitched buzz on the facility and everyone was anxiously awaiting it. The eagerness of this arrival was akin to our excitement today over the new iPhone or maybe concert tickets. If we didn't have to work, I am sure individuals would have camped out. The soda did arrive as scheduled and in cruel fashion that evening, one of my fellow service members was cleaning his grenade launcher and negligently discharged it towards the PX. This potentially catastrophic incident luckily harmed no one, but the horror that was experienced when the smoke cleared was readily apparent. Someway, somehow this round struck our container of soda on the very day it arrived and before it could be put out for sale. It was a total loss. There was a lot of swearing on base that night and the responsible party was quickly removed from the country. In the grand scheme of things, this soda meant nothing, other than a potential break. An opportunity to close your eyes and drink something familiar and daydream that you were anywhere other than here. We would have to save that for another day.

So, with little to no options to purchase items, this meant that everything relied on getting mailed into the country. Since there wasn't much available airlift space on military aircraft, the government contracted mail delivery to third parties. With this came the introduction of DHL. I had heard of FedEx and UPS, but never DHL, and it seemed to me to be a new fly-by-night operation. The planes they flew were old, white, and dirty. They did have the familiar red letters that you see today (without the yellow bodies), and I am fairly certain that I never saw a plane land or take off where one or more of the engines wasn't spewing smoke. The look of the planes meant little to me, as my mail could have flown in a dumpster with wings and I would have been happy to have it. I only bring it up because of how far DHL's business has come since then. I hold a special admiration for DHL today because of some of those early deliveries and the crazy pilots who flew them.

Mail meant the world to us and it was extra special to me. Up until this point my mother had always played a vital role in my life, but when I got the call to go overseas, her support of me became like nothing I could have ever imagined. She went to the post office each week and lied through her teeth on each and every post office declaration form in order to send me items to ease my time there. Running the ammunition supply point, I was right beside the airfield, so I saw every time one of these planes landed. I didn't get a package from every mail delivery plane, but I would have to say that my average was above fifty percent. Some planes brought me none, some brought me one, and some brought me more than one package. It was amusing to see the post marks and how many items arrived out of order in boxes that looked like they had seen better days. If I had received these packages at my house, I would have filed complaints at the local post office, but these were special packages because they had literally been through war and all I really cared about was what was inside. I was like a three-year-old on Christmas morning each time I opened one and that magic never faded away.

CARRIER PIGEONS

MAIL BROUGHT US STUFF, and it was cool and all, but more importantly, it helped connect us to home. This was what we all longed for, and it helped us get through our daily struggles. My wife and I recently just finished binge-watching *Game of Thrones* and I couldn't help but pay special attention to the laser-like precision of message delivery from kingdom to kingdom with the ravens that they deployed. While this is fictional in nature, it reminded me of the frustration of trying to stay connected all those years ago, and for whatever reason, it made me laugh a little.

I'm not sure about the other branches of service, but the Army conditions soldiers early on in basic training about the frustration of trying to make a phone call, and it never lets up. Almost twenty-two years later it's not difficult at all for me to still visualize the bank of pay phones and the excitement of making a Sunday phone call home. In those days, long distance calls were still a real thing and pre-paid phone cards were required to stay connected. Each soldier had ten minutes from the time they touched the phone until the time they hung up, with a watchful drill sergeant maintaining a stopwatch and continually letting you know how much time you had left to the point of distraction. With such a short period of time, the stress of entering an 800 number, pin number, and final destination number while getting screamed at felt at times like it rose to the stress level of diffusing a bomb, which was only relieved when you heard another voice on the other end of the line.

Fast forward four years and there I sat in line at a Morale, Welfare, and Recreation (MWR) tent in Afghanistan, waiting in line to use a phone, shuffling from seat to seat until it was my turn. This time, the stopwatch of the always angry drill sergeant had been replaced by a phone that had an automatic ten minute shut-off. The phones that we used were on the Defense Switched Network (DSN) and they included an extra ripple. I had to call a location in the States and get them to connect me to a morale line. In many ways it would have been easier to go back to the old trusty pre-paid phone card and all of its associated steps. But there was one caveat to this: if I was lucky enough to find a location that was a local call to my final destination, then all I had to do was ask for an outside line and then make my call. There was a whole catalog of DSN numbers that we would scroll through. Each time we would find a good number was like hitting the jackpot, and service members would actually steal the pages that listed these prime locations. The reason behind this was that as soon as a number was considered good, it got abused by the entire base population, and seemingly within days no one answered the phone anymore. Finding a good number was like shooting at a moving target.

The only thing that made any of this bearable was finally hearing the sweet sound of a familiar voice on the other end of the line. That said, there was usually a delay in the call that seemed a lot like a really bad echo and caused me many times to talk over others. Being someone that speaks quickly and reacts quickly, the calls themselves could be exasperating, but honestly the information that was conveyed didn't matter most of the time. The simple assurance that I was okay for friends and family and the voice that I heard was enough to satisfy everyone.

I've never been a patient person, but I waited in these lines more than I cared to do. The entire base did, including various soldiers from other countries. We were briefed repeatedly to be very conscious of them, as there was an urban legend spread that due to a frustration of waiting for calls, two Korean service members had gotten in a fight. In this tale, the senior officer of the two had shot his subordinate and killed him. The story continued that the officer was removed from the country immediately and had to fly home, escorting the remains and he was never heard from again. I can't confirm anything from this story, but it was enough to keep everyone polite and amicable in those long cumbersome lines.

Email in those days was sporadic, and letters could take weeks to arrive, so these few, short, delayed conversations were all that we had. These calls did provide small windows to the outside world and that was something that we all yearned for, friends and family back home included. A lot of my decisions that drove my phone call regimen were for me, but in many situations, it was more for the person thousands of miles away on the other end of the line. One case in point was Christmas. While yes, I did want to talk to my family that had gathered for the holiday, I could have pushed my chat a day or two either way and still met the festive intent. This would have been an easy decision for me, since patience isn't my strongest virtue and the lines were at a historically high level, as one would imagine. All that rationale given, the reason that I rose at two o'clock that early morning was because my mom's birthday was Christmas Day and the only gift that I could physically give her was the sound of my voice. I would have sacrificed a ton to make that call. She was my rock while I was there, and I needed to be hers also.

QUID PRO QUO

I HAVE ALREADY LAID OUT how hard it was to get comfort items and to stay connected in general while in Afghanistan. These struggles didn't dampen anyone's needs or desires, they just made each of us more resourceful in acquisition. Quid pro quo became our official currency. Nowadays, we are getting closer to a cashless world. In fact, on most days I rarely ever have any cash in my pocket at all. That is mainly because I don't need it, but also because I have kids, so if I have any money sitting out on the kitchen counter, they believe the *finders keepers* rule applies and it's gone. Our current cashless world is a recent phenomenon and lends more to the rise of credit cards, debit cards, and direct deposit. Rewinding back to Afghanistan, and for an entirely different reason, getting accustomed to a world without money was difficult. That's not to say that you couldn't carry around money, it just didn't really serve any purpose. With limited buying options, large quantities of cash could only lead to temptations to buy things one didn't need or that might break General Order Number 1. Even the process of acquiring cash felt suspect, as it required waiting in line at the military finance office in order to request a payroll deduction to get money, which felt like a payday loan advance. There was one other ripple too: there were no coins. Whether it was because the weight of coins made them hard to transport or for whatever other reason, I have no clue, even cash purchases at the PX got change returned in a currency they called POGs. Basically, the military had printed and distributed a different currency, mind you one with a cash equivalent, to its service members. These paper coins had the same impact to me as receiving pennies these days, and I am fairly certain that I never actually cashed in a single POG, nor did any of my fellow soldiers. To us, they weren't worth the paper they were printed on.

This seems like a long path to lead one down to discuss the fact that without money, outside our standard daily mission, everything we did was a barter, of sorts. The term *quid pro quo* in my early days in the military had always been used in discussions of sexual harassment, so it obviously had a bad connotation. In recent times, it has gotten a lot of publicity with the impeachment of President Trump as an inherently negative aspect of his dealings with Ukraine. By its nature though, *quid pro quo* simply means "this for that." I will exchange my money or goods or services for yours. If I determine that the *juice is worth the squeeze*, I will do it. On Bagram Airfield, in the early stages of the conflict, I had a lot of cards in my hand that I could use for making deals. I had large rough-terrain fork trucks, a skilled maintenance force, and large trucks to load things on. I also had a lot of soldiers that had attained civilian skills that could help in standing up this new operating base.

Never did I do anything unethical with this hand that I was dealt, but I exchanged my capabilities at will in an effort to improve the lives of my soldiers. I used my trucks and forklifts to help set up force protection with the base provost marshal (police officers) and in exchange, we always got to provide extra security for shopping trips into the local town. I spent several nights in a row helping receive, store, and inspect Italian ammunition when it arrived in theater. In exchange, we had an open invitation for four to five soldiers for lunch everyday (to be completely transparent, I got to be their escort).

This is not to say that we would not help people with their abnormal requests without getting something in return. We did that a lot too. It's more to discuss the relationships that were built by working as a team and the give and take associated with it. Plus, at times, these deals had unintended positive consequences.

In another arrangement with the provost marshal, I was asked to store confiscated Afghani weapons (AK-47s) in my secure ASP. This is a non-standard request that would never happen in the States, but it was critical for the provost marshal. The stockpiles that they had obtained were enough to fill nearly two, twenty-foot storage containers and they were still working the logistics of demolition. This cache of weapons could have instantly armed an enemy and the provost marshal didn't have adequate bandwidth to provide security around the clock, which I did. There was really no benefit in this, except maybe a front row seat to watch the destruction down the road, but I volunteered to help out because it was the right thing to do. Little did I know that this stockpile of weapons could help me with my guard force staff.

I was responsible for overall security of the ASP, where we had four primary tenants: the US Army, Marines, Air Force, and the British Army. I maintained security on day shift, but at night, each tenant unit provided two individuals to provide an overall eight-man guard force. As simple as this sounds, there was one large caveat. All of the US forces fell under a common Rules of Engagement (ROE), while the British Army did not. Our ROE stated that any perceived enemy force inside our perimeter could be considered hostile and engaged immediately with lethal force. The British ROE, on the other hand, required that they physically witness the enemy as armed and preparing to engage before they could respond with deadly force. This difference to some may not seem like much, but being on the outer perimeter of the base, I needed everyone on the same sheet of music in order to protect my soldiers, our assets, and the base as a whole. My answer to the British soldiers was simple: treat every suspicious person inside the perimeter as an armed and engaged enemy combatant. If it turned out that they didn't have a weapon inside our perimeter, they should call me after they shot them and I would make sure they had a weapon, as I had access to a stockpile. This may sound terrible to many, but this was Afghanistan and not the US Criminal Justice system, where I would never condone that behavior. It was based off of maintaining our survival. Luckily, I never had to explore this option with the British soldiers, but I sure as hell would have if required.

That was a very serious example of the relationships and partnerships that you build through quid pro quo, but for the most part these dealings were lighthearted. My most memorable quid pro quo could have easily doubled as a Coca-Cola commercial. As I have already written, soda was a premium on the base, and for the first several months there was none to be had. After a while, the dining facility did start getting a stockpile, but each service member was limited in what they could carry out the door. Through some work-related *drug deals*, we had an insider who could get us some soda for special events. We didn't abuse these connections for personal gain; instead we leveraged it to get additional work done, including engineering work from the Thai Army. Yes, you read that correctly, we traded Coca-Cola for engineering site work.

Like every military deployment, engineering assets were at a premium and they had a long list of priorities, with force protection being first. At the ASP, we were attempting to get a certified operating license through the Department of Defense and had to complete a significant amount of earth-moving to make this happen. We were getting some support but not nearly enough to meet our objective until one day our first sergeant met someone from the Thai Army that could speak just enough English to broker a deal. They basically agreed to exchange a day's work for a dump truck, front end loader, and a roller in exchange for a case of Coke. This may have been the deal of the decade, for both parties. The Thai engineers completed their work on a blistering hot day as requested, so at the end of the workday we stopped by to *pay* them for their efforts. All other movements stopped and everyone came together as the Thai leader passed out their reward. The next few moments felt as if they moved in slow motion as each service member cracked open their ice-cold, refreshing beverage, turned them up in the air and enjoyed the fruits of their labor. Each person in near harmony completed their first long, sweet drink and let out an audible "Ahhhh." It was absolutely priceless and also made me want to give them more. The work they completed was to standard and helped us complete our overall goal, which made all efforts a mutually beneficial quid pro quo.

A GOOD MEAL

I HAVE MADE SOME REFERENCES previously to meals, the importance of which can't be understated, as food is the ultimate comfort for many. It is the centerpiece of nearly every gathering with family and friends. Breaking bread with others is something that is sewn into the fabric of our country and helps define who we are. Worldwide, it is a large part of nearly every culture. And nowadays, meal options and eating out provide abundant choices. If I did a quick search on my phone, there are probably over twenty culinary options within five miles of my house, and that number is constantly evolving and growing. Homestyle cooking, wings, Chinese, Mexican, every type of cuisine is represented. If that weren't enough, there are also two full grocery stores within the same driving range. There are a lot of food options that one could easily take for granted.

Meals in the military are something entirely different. We are indoctrinated into this right away in basic training, where I not-so-fondly remember getting seven minutes to eat from the time the last person sat down at our communal table (that felt anything but). This was not that big a deal if I was at the front of the line, but really sucked when it was my turn to be last. Most meals with friends and family involve robust conversation and maybe some laughter and tears. In contrast, there were probably a few tears, but never any laughter at these basic training meals. Speaking was forbidden, but I honestly don't know who would have had the time to talk as we were shoveling as much as we could into our mouths in the time provided. The moral of this story is that we were shown that food is a necessity for survival and not necessarily a luxury.

That all being said, whenever situations permit eating something different, service members jump all over the opportunity for a good meal. I remember food delivery services to military installations as early as my technical training twenty-plus years ago. This wasn't just the standard pizza or Chinese food delivery. These were booming delivery businesses around the military installation way before DoorDash and Grubhub were ever thought of.

After basic training and technical training and throughout a myriad of training exercises, I thought I had gotten accustomed to Army chow. Even in our time at Fort Lewis, we had no kitchen to prepare food, so the dining facility was our only choice other than junk for several months. In addition to the standard military dining facility rations, I also had consumed my fair share of meals ready to eat (MREs), to the point that the novelty had worn off of them. I say that because when I first joined the Army, I, like everyone, was excited about eating MREs and I stayed excited about them until I had to eat them for three meals a day for several days in a row. With the intestinal distress that this caused, having to consume MREs was hoped to be the exception, not the norm.

As we arrived in Afghanistan, our meal schedule was tolerable, with two hots (breakfast and dinner) and an MRE for lunch each day. Due to logistical constraints on the base, there were no *reefer* vans when I first arrived, which meant there was no refrigerated storage. So while breakfast and dinner promised hot meals, they turned out to be one small step above MREs, as they provided the same meal options, just warmed up by someone else. I guess this is what ketchup, hot sauce, and salt were designed to mask. Even once the reefer vans arrived on base, the only food option that they provided was chicken cordon bleu, which I don't particularly like. After several months of eating from a can or a bag boiled in water, the thought of chicken cordon bleu was tantalizingly and I ate every crumb. And then we had it for dinner the next day and the next day. I believe it was served as a dinner option for something like five straight days, which was long enough for me to remember that I really didn't like chicken cordon bleu in the first place.

With our dining facility not providing much for options, this is where the story gets interesting. Looking back, it is crazy to think of the lengths that soldiers, myself included, would go to get a good meal. In fact, we never had a shortage of volunteers to leave the safety of the base to complete a mission that promised something different to eat at the end. Growing up in West Virginia, cleaning a weapon to hunt something to consume was common for a lot of friends and family. For most, it was more the sport of the hunt than the fruits of the kill. I did it a few times myself, but after a few trips, decided it was not worth the early mornings and freezing cold. In comparison to these efforts, Afghanistan brought with it, early mornings, weapons cleaning, several hundred rounds of ammo, body armor and long drives through the countryside to get ourselves to a good meal. Most of our trips were from Bagram to Kabul, where I vividly remember a sunken pass on the drive that had random speed bumps that appeared in a location that would have been ripe for an ambush. We never encountered any issues like that on any of our trips, but then again, we never slowed down to find out. Driving an SUV, this wasn't that big a deal, but we were always followed by a large truck that transported palletized loads that had an air suspension. I did many trips in the lead vehicle where as soon as we flew across the speed bumps, ala *The Dukes of Hazzard*, we would instantly look in the rearview mirror to see the passenger of that truck flying into the air when they hit the speed bumps. I also did several trips in the trail vehicle where they don't make an *oh shit handle* big enough to help keep you down. This whole scenario was dangerous as hell, but in the moment, I didn't notice it. A little later, I'll get into a battle that my chief and I had over ammunition deliveries to Kabul. While those were high priority missions for us, they also included a hot meal at the US Embassy with the State Department, so for me they reduced the reluctance and frustration that those trips caused.

As crazy as it may sound, running the risk of getting shot or blown up to get a decent meal was probably not the dumbest thing I did to try to eat well. I believe that honor is reserved for the times I ate food from the locals, particularly the bread. I don't know what created this appeal, it certainly wasn't watching the artisans knead the dough with unwashed hands without gloves or watching the bread bake in the hot Afghani sun, in a dirty environment. There was nothing rational about the desire to eat it, but it was fresh bread, and most of us did it. I must admit, it was delicious, but also very hard on my stomach. But that didn't stop me from doing it over and over again. The impact on my stomach lessened each time.

Food is a central tenant in a lot of what I share here and figures prominently in my memories of my time in Afghanistan. Food brought comfort, something all of us were longing for.

PART III: THE GOOD STUFF

On the darkest day there's always light and now I see it too.
—Clint Black

AN AFGHANI THANKSGIVING DAY FEAST WITH A FAKE BUZZ

AFGHANISTAN WAS TOUGH, but when I look back on it, the good parts always come to mind first. It was the greatest military experience of my career, so I want to share some of the stories that make me smile, even today. As Poison once said though, *every rose has its thorns*, and most things weren't perfect from beginning to end. Hell, at the time, I didn't even know that most experiences would turn out to be roses. These memories have certainly gotten better with age.

I hit boots on ground in September, and I think the best place to start is my first real holiday overseas. It was Thanksgiving Day 2002, and I missed everything about home. We were going on two months of bagged and canned army C rations, which in retrospect is a pretty appropriate grade for the food quality. The lack of fresh food to prepare and eat had been an adjustment, but one all of us were getting accustomed to by that point. With the arrival of this holiday that centers around food, the limited food options were beginning to put a strain on morale. This was tough on me—both as a leader and as a person. Everyone wanted something that resembled a homecooked meal to provide a reprieve on Thanksgiving, even if only for a few short minutes. The local command was working feverishly on the logistics to make it happen, but I was skeptical. I believed that trying to pull this off was about the equivalent of trying to hit a homerun off of Nolan Ryan while using a balloon as a bat.

As the days got closer to this amazing holiday of historical gluttony, the anticipation was starting to build. A few days before the holiday, our base command cell announced that a large hurdle had been cleared: reefer vans were being flown in specifically for the holiday. The announcement proudly proclaimed that we would, in fact, have fresh turkey. At this point, I was starting to get a little more excited, while still staying partially reserved, until the day finally arrived. The day started with an alteration in our meal schedule, as there was no hot breakfast. Instead we were provided with an extended lunch/dinner window. After an MRE that I barely grazed through for breakfast, I worked about a half day until finally it was my time to eat. The line for the dining facility tent was extra-long that day, and it helped build an eagerness that was killing me. I waited for what felt like an eternity in a place where some days felt like entire lifetimes until it was finally my turn. I entered the tent structure and began my ritual of washing my hands at the portable station with no hand soap and cold water. As I peeled back the second tent flap to enter, the first thing that caught my eye were the drink coolers, which were fully stocked with O'Doul's. I have never been a fan of *near beer*, but the sight of this cold, frothy beverage instantly piqued my interest. I grabbed my paper tray and plastic silverware and instantly my nose got its first whiff of our holiday feast. At the start of the serving line, prominently displayed right in front of me was a heat lamp with a fake cooked turkey underneath it. This perfectly prepared, but fake bird looked like something from a commercial and I probably could have convinced myself it eat it at the time. What happened next can only be described as a complete and utter disappointment, although that doesn't do it justice. I looked at the stainless steel pan in front of me at the beginning of the serving line and there it was. Cold cut turkey in Army gravy. Don't get me wrong, I love me some Louis Rich and Butterball lunchmeat, anytime other than Thanksgiving, especially *that* Thanksgiving. I knew the potatoes weren't going to be real, but come on, dammit! Regardless of my near paralyzing disappointment, my tray was filled quickly, and I made a quick beeline to the O'Doul's and grabbed two. Although it wasn't what I really wanted, I ate my Thanksgiving dinner as if I was coming off a two-month hunger strike. Although still stewing from disappointment, I knew it was better than anything that I had devoured recently, so that made it a little better. Once I finished eating, I popped open my pseudo adult beverages and hammered them back. What came next can only be described as pleasantly unpredicted. My belly was full and shockingly, I had a warm feeling that felt a lot like a beer buzz. All I could think was *how the hell was this possible with near beer*? The rationale of my next decision I would like to fully blame on my fake partially impaired state. Like a cartoon character that wasn't in control of my own movements, I found myself gravitating to the beer coolers like I was floating on air. I filled my cargo pockets with as many cans as they would hold. I can't remember what the next activity was that night, whether it was a game of Spades or smoking cheap cigars, but all I recall is that I drank like four more O'Doul's. In my mind, my two-beer buzz was going to be replaced by a good drunk. In reality, my placebo effect buzz was gone. Instead, I was bloated and had to pee repeatedly, which involved a long walk to the aforementioned blue palaces, that were almost filled to the seat by this point in the evening (as with most). Not only was I bloated, but I also had to hold my breath when I entered so as not to taste my disappointing meal on its way back up. I miserably repeated this cycle multiple times throughout the night, pissed off, but knowing the only person that I had to blame was myself. In one stretch of irony though, after about my third trip, I did declare that I was never drinking like that again. I may have never been able to hold that promise as it related to alcohol before, but I had no problem swearing off near beer from that day forward. It didn't take long for all the effects of my day to wear off, and although it wasn't exactly what I wanted, it did provide a good break from the world around me. That is all I really needed.

OPERATION OUTBACK

WHILE THE THANKSGIVING DAY MEAL started with anticipation and ended in disappointment, my best meal experience from my entire deployment began with a fever pitch and ended in agony. It was just after the holidays at the beginning of 2003, when news broke on the base that we had an incredibly special meal coming. Outback Steakhouse had sponsored *Operation Outback* to support the troops deployed overseas. This initiative included shipping steaks, deep fryers, and Bloomin' Onions to soldiers stationed outside of the United States. After the Thanksgiving bait and switch, I will admit I was a little skeptical, but after reviewing some of the logistics operations taking place, I soon realized that this was the real deal. My level of excitement for this compared to our Thanksgiving meal was the equivalent of the night before Christmas compared to the night before a visit to the dentist for children.

The buildup on the base was immense, and by the time the day arrived, everything pretty much had screeched to a standstill. This event was consuming everything. I think the base population may have grown by a few hundred since my arrival, but it seemed like when I took my place in line at the dining facility that night, there were thousands of people in front of me. I peacefully waited my turn although the aroma in the air made me feel like a drooling German Shepherd. The smell of grilling is something that can be taken for granted at home, but after a few months of life overseas, it may have been the sweetest aroma that had ever entered my nose. I waited for what seemed like ages, all the while hoping that they didn't run out of food. I was fairly certain that there was no way that they would have shipped too little food, as we were all heavily armed and that could have led to catastrophe. Soon enough, my fears were put to rest, and it was finally my turn to grab a paper tray and plastic silverware (which is a terrible way to eat steak). Unlike my Thanksgiving experience, the visual of what I encountered once I arrived at the serving line was exactly as advertised. They were serving steak and baked potatoes on the main line. But wait, there were no Bloomin' Onions. I could see people eating them scattered throughout the dining facility, so surely they hadn't run out. Not having a Bloomin' Onion at this meal would have been like unwrapping my last Christmas present and it being a toothbrush. All the other presents were great and all, but a disappointing last present just leaves one unfulfilled.

I snapped out of my unfounded outrage over a fried onion that I had seemingly been deprived of as my group found a couple of empty seats in the packed facility. To my pleasant surprise, no more than two or three minutes passed until a waitress (yes, they sent waitresses too) came around to deliver the piping hot appetizer I was craving. That is when I discovered that the seats we had found open were the equivalent of hitting the binge-eating jackpot. A newfound stranger-turned-friend at the table had been this waitress's security detail the day before, so she kept the onions coming. I began to eat without mercy. And I ate and ate and ate, and when I was full, I ate some more. I put myself in a food coma at the table and got up a bit later feeling fat, dumb, and happy.

As with the near beer scenario from before, my happiness was exceptionally short-lived. The walk back to my tent must have settled the food into my stomach and my lack of a diet involving greasy foods for the last few months came roaring back at me. Over the course of this five-minute walk, I went from bliss to anguish. I had never experienced a pain like this before and my short walk developed into a struggle. All I wanted to do was lie down on my cot and die. As I opened my tent door, I quickly realized that I was not alone. Everyone in the tent was lying on their cot, moaning like newly formed walkers from *The Walking Dead*. Additionally, there was a stench in the tent that resembled a combination of smashed assholes and onions. I laid down and took my position of misery on my cot, where I attempted not to move for a few hours. If anyone had attacked the base during that time, they could have just marched in, as I am fairly certain that no one would have put up any resistance. The anticipation of Outback had brought the base to a halt, but after the meal, we were incapable of restarting. Everyone on base was experiencing a food hangover. Luckily, like all hangovers, the pain was short-lived, relatively speaking, as it didn't feel that way at the time. I briefly doubted my decision making during the peak of my discomfort, but that passed quickly. I would have made the same exact decisions over and over again if given the chance. To this day, I have a fondness for Outback that will never change and I deeply appreciate their continued dedication to this nation's soldiers.

LITTLE THINGS MEAN A LOT

WHILE THE FEW GOOD MEALS that I had in Afghanistan were both positive and memorable, one of the most profound impacts on me while serving was learning to appreciate the little things again. A short while back when I thought that I wanted to start blogging about the military, I composed a list of items that were telltale signs that one was a veteran. I was inspired by Veteran's Day, and the list came to me quite easily. Nearly anyone that has ever served can relate to the items below.

You can sleep anywhere and in any condition. Whether trying to sleep while holding a newspaper up to cover your face or napping on the toilet (this takes skill and a brave soul), you learn how to sleep in any situation.

Your meals have gone from eating what you want to eat to eating whatever they will give you. Growing up, I would not touch a green bean, but when there is nothing to replace it as part of your meal, opinions change.

Condiments are a food group. Seasoning is optional for military cooking, but ketchup and hot sauce are mandatory. I never liked Tabasco sauce before Afghanistan but finding a bottle in my MRE pack was like a little slice of heaven.

You have handwritten a letter. In today's digital world, it is a lost art. Every soldier invests in the Army stationary and sends letters home from basic training.

You have watched bad old TV shows and movies that you would never confess to watching—and loved them. Yes, I admit I watched *Coyote Ugly* more than once and other instant classics like *40 Days and 40 Nights* while in Afghanistan. Never in my life would I watch those films at home, but I enjoyed the hell out of them there.

You have watched a movie filmed by someone watching a movie and at times become pissed off when you realize it was in the wrong language. Three movies on a five-dollar DVD were worth the risk, though.

You have waited in long lines for things you don't really want. Long lines may be ok for concert tickets or black Friday deals, but waiting for shots or meals that taste like cardboard not so much.

You have called a kid sir or ma'am. It's a hard habit to break.

You understand varying standards of cleanliness. Bonus points if you have washed your clothes in a cardboard box.

You have hurried up to wait and that totally makes sense.

You have been on time for something but uncomfortably slunk in as if you were late.

And to be a little more serious....

Hearing TAPS play will make every hair stand up on the back of your neck and most likely brings a tear to your eye.

You understand pride. The only equal to pride in service may be that of your children (hopefully). But without either, I don't think you can truly understand what pride is.

So how is this list relevant? It's actually quite simple: little things mean a lot. My Afghanistan adventure was the inspiration for several items on that list, with the bootleg movies being a prime example. As we would watch each movie fire up, I would complete a mental checklist:

- Is there audio?
- Is it in English?
- If it's not in English, are there subtitles?
- If there are subtitles, is this a movie that I want to watch badly enough to read what is going on?
- Was the film from a legitimate source and not someone filming inside the theater?
- If the movie was filmed by someone sitting in the seats, is it a comedy? If so, all the laughter is filmed and will take away from the movie, so am I willing to put up with that?

Each yes or no answer had either a positive or negative impact on my experience. In most situations, I must admit, I watched the movie anyway.

The item about cleanliness above also rang true from my time in Afghanistan. Between the shower and laundry situation, I was constantly dirty. That was, of course, until I made a fieldtrip to Kandahar, where I believe I had the greatest shower of my entire life—and it was outdoors. I have to give absolute credit to soldiers for being completely resourceful. I originally was skeptical about the shower setup in Kandahar. It made some outhouses I'd seen before look fancy. They had rigged up a fifty-five gallon barrel, immersion heater, pump, and a tarp. Through much experimentation, they had perfected the amount of water to add, the time to turn on the heater before stepping in, and the amount of time they could spend in the shower. They warned me that if I stayed beyond the shower timer they set, the water would get too hot and burn me. I think all told, I was only in the shower about five minutes, but it felt like several amazing hours. When it was over, I put the same dirty, but technically clean clothes back on, but I didn't care. Those five good minutes made up for the rest of the awful night.

Soldier resourcefulness always makes things better. Some of my best memories from Afghanistan involve the pickup basketball games we would play. That's probably not a comment most would expect, but it's very true. For extra force protection, we had a new guard structure delivered that would sit on top of the metal storage connex that we had at the entrance to the ASP. I am not sure where it came from, but a basketball rim and ball showed up right around the same time as the new guard shack. The timing was impeccable, as we were able to mount the rim before the structure had its exterior walls sandbagged. Being made of wood, the guard structure was a perfect backboard. The games we would play were rough, but fun, and I can't count how many times I slammed into the side of the metal connex after a layup or trying to get a rebound. We always stuck to break and lunch periods, but we wore that basketball hoop out. I lost count of the amount of times we replaced the net or had to reweld the rim. Each time it would break, our behavior mimicked that of kids playing basketball in the street, stopping for a car. The game would disperse until the rim was welded back together and we gave it time to cool. Then we were back at it again at the next opportunity.

These little things are what make me smile when I think back on them. They come to mind much faster than any of the negative memories and were a way to balance the struggles of life there.

A MULTINATIONAL FLARE

ANOTHER AMAZING PART of my time overseas was the variety of people I interacted with. The US involvement in Afghanistan was a multinational affair with tons of participation from many of our NATO partners. The irony of all of this was that my time in Afghanistan began in earnest during the buildup of American forces in Iraq. I saw many headlines that showed that most of the nations that I was serving with were condemning potential action in Iraq, or at least publicly. I imagine that many of the private conversations between these world leaders pretty much went something like this:

> George (President Bush), it would be political suicide for me to support your war effort in Iraq, but I would be more than happy to send extra troops to Afghanistan, an effort that my citizens support. This will allow you to put more focus on Iraq and I will help carry the Afghanistan burden. Of course, I will deny this if confronted publicly, but we are good, right?

This multinational effort truly resulted in some of the best moments of my time in Afghanistan. Many of these personal interactions carried with them a lot of preconceived notions and were surely stereotypical, but they made my time great.

THE POLES

MY INTERACTION WITH THE POLISH military effort was in a few short words both awesome and memorable. When I grew up, my uncle was of Polish decent and he told *Polack* jokes one after another, which were pretty much the equivalent of all the old-school dumb blonde jokes. Nearly every interaction that I had with the Polish Army there provided some takeaway that made me smile and reminded me of these terribly inappropriate jokes.

The most memorable of all my accounts of the Polish Army involved the mine clearing team. They literally walked through mine fields. They would roll up to their work site in two vehicles with roughly twelve soldiers and ten chairs. Ten people would watch and two people would work. This job bordered on insanity. These crazy sons of bitches would put on special, big floppy shoes and then walk around a mine field, marking land mines. These shoes somehow helped balance their weight and did not cause the land mines to detonate. I cannot believe the confidence they had in their equipment. I mentioned the ten people on break and two people working as something that seemed strange, but honestly after watching them work, ninety-nine people could have watched while one person worked and I would not have complained. There is no way in hell I would sign up for that job.

Including this mine sweeping group, the Polish engineers were interesting as a whole. Being in charge of the ASP, each tenant unit on the base had to store their explosives at my site. We provided a courtesy storage of their munitions that we gave them access to around the clock. The only thing that we asked for was a copy of their inventory so that we could try to find the safest way to store it. Most unit's munitions were operational in nature, so there wasn't too much explosive weight. The Polish munitions were different. Their inventory was to support their engineering mission, and they had a staggering number of Bangalore torpedoes, which were used to help detonate mines. I still remember the conversation with one of their officers where I tried to explain that they had enough explosives to turn the entire base into a crater. He simply laughed, as he thought that was a good thing. I explained to him that I could not store it all at our site and that he had to move some around to spread out the risk, which after much prodding, he agreed to do. Getting to this victory was significant due to our language barrier and our differences in rationale.

This relationship with the Poles carried on further, as they did some engineering work for me. Their efforts were both helpful and frustrating. The two gentlemen that came out to perform the work were sergeants in the Polish Army, which I was told meant that they only worked half a day each. And that is all I ever saw. One would show up in the morning driving a front end loader and would leave at lunchtime. His replacement would bring the same piece of construction equipment back in the afternoon. I had a lot of work for them to do, as previously mentioned, I was trying to acquire a storage capacity license from the Department of Defense to transform this contingency ammunition holding site to a safer, longer term solution. This meant I needed a lot of barricades built and dirt moved. But despite their unusual workday, all was going well with this group until the day my Polish team got in their heads that they needed to dig a tunnel for me, the *big boss*, because "everyone needs a tunnel." I am sure my soldiers had something to do with it, and I thought they were joking at first, until they started trying to dig. I passionately stopped them, which I believe offended the operator, who gruffly informed me that the truck was broken and that he would be back tomorrow. As pissed as I was by this halting of all the work, I had no recourse, as they were helping the US forces out. After that day, I decided to agree to have a tunnel built, just once we finished the other work that had to get done on the base. I had no idea where the tunnel would go, but I was fairly certain that once I said that all required engineering work was complete that they would not be back to dig any longer so promising he could build a tunnel didn't have too much risk. I just wondered how I got to that point in the first place.

All the interaction with the Poles got me and my soldiers invited to tour and hang out in their compound. I humbly accepted and several of my soldiers and I went to explore. Once there, we were immediately invited to participate in a volleyball game, which seemed harmless enough. Harmless, until that is, we stepped onto the court, where we were greeted by what seemed like the Polish Olympic National Volleyball team. I had played my fair share of volleyball in the past, but my skills were frankly a lot closer to family-reunion level than even junior varsity level at this time. After probably the third spike was buried at my feet with laser precision, I started having high school gym class flashbacks of our instructor yelling, "bump, set, spike!" I snapped out of that mindset quickly, abandoning the idea that employing those tactics would enable us to battle our way back. Instead, we just got killed.

Part of the issue during the volleyball game may have been the distraction that occurred when I looked on the roof of their housing and saw at least five Polish soldiers standing in a circle talking. I inquired about what I saw, and through a broken translation was told that their satellite dish was broken and they had lost access to porn. There were two surprising points to this answer. One was the obvious part about porn and the fact that we were not allowed to view any. The other, more astonishing, part was that I had never seen more than two Polish soldiers work at a time and here I was witnessing five of them, elbow-deep trying to fix their satellite dish. I was smiling from ear to ear.

THE BRITISH

MY INTERACTIONS WITH THE BRITS were nowhere near as outlandish as the Poles, but that doesn't make them any less memorable. The small contingent force of British soldiers that ran their portion of the ASP was basically a nested part of our unit. While they had their own chain of command, they were operationally controlled for the most part by my unit command team. Our relationship with them was so close that they even stayed in the same tent block with us just two short doors down.

This small team of three Brits provided a frequent, much-needed reprieve for me. After getting my work team started most mornings, I headed to the British command tent for morning tea and satellite British television news. Yes, that's correct, my connection to the outside world was a satellite dish located in the British Army's tent. Here, I learned important lessons about opening my ears to listen as part of looking at both sides of an issue. I was fully supportive of my mission in Afghanistan and even believed in the need to build up troops in Iraq. I spent many a morning with my British staff sergeant debating the merits of a full-on Iraq war and the impact on the international community. Even with the British being our staunchest ally, there was some reluctance to agree that going into Iraq was the right thing to do. All that considered, the staff sergeant always stated that the British would be side by side with us. The significance of that was pretty awesome. For me, the whole relationship between me and my British counterparts was fantastic, as it allowed me to become a little more than just Lieutenant Warner to them, although I didn't necessarily want to go by their nickname for me, the *Ginger Ninja*.

THE ITALIANS

THAT WHOLE SECTION in my introduction to this chapter about moving troops to Afghanistan so that US soldiers could go to Iraq summed up the Italian Army in a nutshell. No one ever expressly stated this to me, but it was a poorly kept secret. In the news coverage that I saw (with the Brits), I watched how the Italian government was condemning our involvement in Iraq. At the same time, I got tasked with a mission to support the Italian Army's arrival into Afghanistan. My function was to receive multiple planeloads of Italian ammunition onto the airfield and to set up temporary, safe storage for it until it moved on to its final destination. These loads, like many, arrived in the middle of the night, so I had multiple sleepless nights in a row to complete this mission. While a large inconvenience for me, completing this mission greatly aided the welfare of my soldiers because I built an immediate relationship with an Italian Officer, Lieutenant Walter (no clue what his last name was), when he arrived. This relationship garnered us an open invitation to join the Italians for lunch each day.

I still remember the first time that I arrived at their compound and the smell of fresh baked bread that overwhelmed me. I found out quickly that the Italian military didn't travel without their ovens. This further confirmed what I already knew, which was that many of our sister countries certainly traveled better than we did. The Poles had their porn, the British had their satellite news, and the Italians had their bread ovens and, I soon found out, their espresso machines as well. That's right, after an amazing meal of freshly made pasta and bread, we finished our lunch off with a hot, delicious espresso. I was never much for coffee before this time, but one could have referred to this as *nectar of the gods* and I would not have disagreed.

The food and drink shared with the Italians was amazing, but it didn't quite make up for the near heart attack that I had while in country that I briefly mentioned at the beginning of the book, regarding the prohibition of alcohol for US troops. The day before I was supposed to leave Lieutenant Walter came by with some food to help us celebrate our departure. The box he brought was full of bread, salami, cheese, and two glorious bottles of wine. There was no way I was going to tempt fate and get caught drinking with less than twenty-four hours to go, so I immediately told Walter to take it away. I appreciated the gesture, but I just couldn't do it.

The food was amazing though, and I spent my last night in country with a full belly, reflecting on my time there and the perfect friendships and partnerships that I had developed. Afghanistan was dirty and rough, but I also loved getting to experience some European culture through my new friendships. I had tea with the British, coffee with the Italians, and played volleyball with the Poles. I had countless other adventures with many other services and countries. These are a big part of the reason that I look back on my time there fondly.

AN OBSESSION WITH RUNNING

FOOD WAS A PREDOMINANT WAY of helping us escape, but it wasn't the most typical of how you cope in the military. That distinction was reserved for running. It was crazy to me how quickly we got into a stateside type regiment as it related to physical fitness, because frankly, it's the only life we know.

One of the early memories I have from basic training (even though it's been twenty years) was the stratification of run groups. They broke us down into five groups based off our run times, but Army basic training is only made up of three types of soldiers, as it relates to running. There are those in the fast group, those that want to be in the fast group, and those that are praying daily just to pass. The military sets expectations up front that an ability to run is a rite of passage. This was reinforced further when I became an officer, where the expectation was that you would lead from the front and the only way to do that was to be able to run. This was a shallow judgment of leadership, but one that was utilized, nonetheless.

I stress these points to explain the insane rationale to hold a marathon in Afghanistan on the day after Thanksgiving in 2002. To illustrate the lunacy behind this, the air quality was horrendous (trash and shit from our base were being burned not too far off post), the walking surfaces were hazardous (there was a road and a sidewalk and a ditch in between that we were still finding land mines in when I left the country), and there was no effective way to train. The options for running on the base were: braving the workout tent that had a year's worth of sweat and funk soaked into the canvas walls, running the base perimeter with a rifle, or running on the main artery of the base, a mile-and-a-half-long stretch of road we called *Disney Drive*. I liken running on Disney Drive to the view of a sled dog: unless you are in front, the scenery never changes. Well, I didn't have anything in front of me, but running up and down a pothole-filled road dodging at least a dozen Humvees per run was about as appealing as staring at a dog's ass. But I still did it six to seven times a week.

I was on the fence about participating in this debacle, but being a reservist in an active duty world, I didn't know that I could say no. Peer pressure was a real thing. To make matters worse, I had run nearly every morning since I arrived in country and I started to develop shin splints, so I had to take several days off to let my legs recover. Even this didn't deter me. Woefully unprepared, I found myself milling around the starting line on a cool November morning, wondering what the hell was I thinking. We had armed guards staged around the base, so running the outside perimeter wouldn't require a weapon. The run course was simple; we had to make the base loop a little over four times. I was dreading the run, but I will admit I was nervously excited. I was turning this into a personal challenge. I had done a few 10K races previously and I decided to challenge myself once with a fifteen mile distance run, but fifteen miles was my longest run ever (including my training for this marathon). As I looked around, not surprisingly there were dozens of other participants ready to start. I am sure some were there because they truly wanted to be, and others experienced a little bit of the same pressure I received to be there. Regardless, we would have this story to share together. It would be pretty badass to personally say that I ran a marathon in a war zone.

The run itself was pretty uneventful, except for two occurrences that struck me as odd. The first was running behind an officer from the British Army who I noticed in front of me almost changing his running form to that of trying to straddle a line. It wasn't long until I noticed the line on the ground and realized that he was peeing. This was the *Mine Field Marathon*, not the Boston Marathon and this guy was actually peeing in front of me. I was running about a four-hour pace to finish, so I was in the rear. I couldn't fathom how this guy seriously could not take a two minute bathroom break. Being toward the back with me it wasn't as if he was jeopardizing his win.

The second item that wasn't normal involved me. I have always been the guy who won't eat anything before a workout, but holy crap, eighteen miles in I would have eaten an entire steak dinner if it was in front of me. My level of hunger was so bad that I broke off the run course, ran back to my tent, and grabbed a snickers bar. I guess it was a good thing that it wasn't the Boston Marathon.

All told, I ran just over a four hour marathon and was rewarded with Army food and I had to walk upstairs backwards for a day or two. It was a great experience for me, but to this day, I still don't see the rationale behind the event, other than publicity. I found out a few weeks after the marathon that the event had been covered in a couple of papers back in the States, so it was pretty cool for my family to see a glimpse of what I was doing, and it was something we could share. This goes back to how sweet the little things are.

PRETTY GIRLS, SUPERSTARS, AND POLITICIANS

A LOT OF WHAT I HAVE DISCUSSED so far revolves around the best things in Afghanistan and items that kill time and got our minds off of the everyday situation. Perhaps the best reprieve of all was provided by the Uniformed Services Organization (USO). The USO is an extraordinary organization that does amazing work for service members around the globe, from airport lounges to deployed getaways. I don't think that I have ever heard a fellow soldier utter a negative word about the USO. One of the services that the USO is famous for is providing entertainment shows to soldiers. During my time in Afghanistan, I met comedians, rock icons, and professional cheerleaders. In most cases, my attendance was not because I was truly a fan of whoever was visiting. Most times it was my best (aka only) option. Plus, as I previously described when I wrote about tent living and Afghanistan, my threshold of entertainment was severely diminished and I probably would have showed up to watch a performance by New York City subway station drummers (who by the way are very talented). This also goes back to the description of being a veteran and having waited in line for hours for things I really didn't want. I did just that to meet Joan Jett after her performance and to get her autograph.

Like seriously, I knew one of her songs, what was I going to do with this signed piece of dirty paper?

The same can't be said for the cheerleaders from the team then known as the Washington Redskins. I gladly waited in line for those photos and autographs. Ironically, the value of these autographs would be significantly less than that of Joan Jett, but I didn't care. I was just happy they came because, if nothing else, they didn't smell like the desert.

The highlight of all the visitors in my time overseas was Robin Williams (Rest in Peace). I was fully expecting *Mrs. Doubtfire*-level comedy and got something a lot closer to Eddie Murphy from his *Raw* days. It was hilarious and a little raunchy. As a bonus, there is video footage of me in the background snapping photos with an old school Kodiak disposable camera while he performs (https://www. youtube.com/watch?v=MArdJ9Kku4E). For security reasons, no one reported on Robin Williams being in Afghanistan until after he was gone, but it was awesome when the story hit the news and my family got to see me doing well with a smile on my face.

In addition to the USO shows, I also got the privilege of meeting two members of the US Senate, Jay Rockefeller of West Virginia and John Warner of Virginia. They pulled aside service members from their respective states and we had a town hall-type discussion. They addressed issues that really mattered to us, including retirement, benefits, and the Iraq conflict, which was kicking off at that time. When it was nearing the end, Senator Rockefeller asked for a pen and paper and requested that each of us write down our home telephone numbers. He told us he wanted to reach out and speak to our parents or spouses. I remember thinking, *yeah right, he's probably going to have a staff member do it*, but to my surprise, a few weeks later when I spoke to my mother, she told me about speaking to Senator Rockefeller. My grandmother, who had passed a few years earlier, loved Senator Rockefeller and we fondly discussed how proud that would have made her to know that he had called to talk about her grandson. I found that to be pretty awesome, myself. He didn't do it as any form of a publicity stunt. He just took time out of his busy day to tell my mother that he had met me and that I was doing okay.

Rockefeller was a Democrat and Warner was a Republican, but there was no partisanship in their visit. There were a few pictures snapped, but nothing to be used in a campaign ad, and that's a good thing. Reflecting back on their time in Afghanistan led me back to some thoughts I had written at the end of 2018 after President Trump visited Germany and Iraq, and it shows the stark contrast in narrative (plus it gives a shoutout to Joan Jett and the cheerleaders).

PLEASE KEEP THE US MILITARY OUT OF THE POLITICAL DIVIDE

The America that I loved is fractured along partisan lines. Each side of the political divide is led by polarizing figures that continue to pull away in their respective direction, seemingly leaving a larger gap in between. A lot has been made recently about the president's visit to Iraq and Germany to visit US service members. He has been lauded by some and crucified by others, with each side spinning a narrative about the thoughts and behavior of the US military to the president. I am imploring everyone to leave our service members out of the politics; we cannot pick a side. We are the one group that must remain in the middle. When you join the military, you take an oath that charges you with two critical things. First, you swear that you will *support and defend the constitution of the United States* and second, you promise that you will *obey the orders of the president of the United States and the orders of the officers appointed over me.* This oath puts each service member in a unique position. The president is our commander in chief, the CEO of the military. We serve at the discretion of the president, whether they are liberal or conservative. We must cheer for his or her success.

President George H.W. Bush recently passed away and a lot has been made about the letter he left for President Bill Clinton as he was leaving office. He closed his letter by stating "You will be our president when you read this note. I wish you well. I wish your family well. Your success now is our country's success. I am rooting hard for you." His graciousness, even after a bitter defeat, is a model for all to follow that, in today's political atmosphere, will never happen. As an American, I know that we should all cheer for our president, but that expectation is lost, possibly forever. I beg everyone to allow the military to remain neutral. We must continue to root for our service members entrenched in this middle ground. Their success is most certainly imperative for the success of our nation.

The media's narrative of Trump's visit to service members overseas at Christmas was simply put, disappointing—on both sides of the aisle. While probably not the best decision by some of the soldiers to bring their MAGA attire to the Iraq event, it was far from a malicious political rally. They are in Iraq, where dress options are whatever the hell they issued you, followed by whatever you're allowed to wear. In some situations, they issue you uniforms that they don't even let you wear. My point is, I don't care that a service member saw Trump in Iraq while wearing their uniform and neither should you. Shame on the conversation of a possible violation of regulation. As a service member, getting visitors overseas is a reminder of the great things at home and a reprieve from the stress of the day to day. I met Joan Jett and the Washington Redskins cheerleaders in Afghanistan. I have no idea why, but I waited in line to have a picture taken with both in my uniform. I can assure you that in no way was this a military endorsement.

These same media outlets are making a big deal about the actions of our last two presidents visiting military members at Christmas. Let me stop that narrative here. President Obama visiting US Marines in Hawaii every year while on vacation does nothing to impress me. And President George W. Bush visiting service members at Walter Reid Army Medical Center at Christmas is akin to showing up at church on Christmas and Easter. It isn't enough to come twice a year; you must exhibit the behavior year-round. Let me be clear, I appreciate my last two commanders in chief and have no issues with them. I'm just trying to stress my point that this skewed comparison of our current president to that of his predecessors is ridiculous.

On the other side of the aisle, I don't need conservative commentators telling me how much these service members love their president. This opinion would seemingly be supported by a recent AP poll that discussed the votes cast by service members at the November midterms and the approval ratings for Trump from veterans (https://www.apnews.com/3b0264d3b4db4c899d98ab3df9 902fe4). Let me take the spin away from this. Most military members I have met over the last twenty years are by nature conservative and pro-gun. Our perception is that a Republican government will yield better pay raises and benefits, but that doesn't mean we won't support the Democratic party. We love and support the United States and have committed to give the ultimate sacrifice, if necessary, to support it against all enemies, foreign or domestic. Simply put, we cheer for our country.

The bottom line is that we serve at the pleasure of the president, a relationship that I feel should be revered, not propagandized or exploited. We are his or her knights, not pawns. No matter what party controls the White House, we are their fighting force. There are no Republican platoons or Democrat platoons. The future of our nation depends on service members staying that way.

PORN RESEARCH

ALL THAT I'VE TOUCHED ON so far that was good in my time revolved around items that were sanctioned and therefore appropriate. The last two items that made my time bearable were neither. They weren't illegal either. They just stayed in the gray area, which made them all the more appealing.

As I have already harped upon, General Order Number 1 prohibited the possession and viewing of pornography. This wasn't something that as a leader I was really searching out, though. It was almost like another version of the *don't ask, don't tell* policy, which was why it was surprising to me when my soldiers approached me at work and informed me that they had found an ammunition container full of pornographic materials. This was probably more to save their own asses in the event that we found it later, but I do remember simply telling them to dispose of the materials. I wasn't overly interested in physically watching them get rid of the items.

Regardless, the possession of pornography, if discovered would get you in trouble. One thing that could compound this punishment would be to view it on a government-owned computer or on a government network. I thought this was common sense but, as I have learned many times in the Army, common sense isn't always too common. Several years later, I was assigned to an Army Reserve unit with a gentleman who worked for the federal government who found the temptation to view porn while traveling too great. He said he knew it was wrong, but he couldn't stop. Well, it stopped him. He lost his job and his federal pension, and I have no idea how he explained it to his wife. He wasn't dismissed from the military because the incident was unrelated to his Reserve job, but it did negatively impact him.

Rewind back to Afghanistan, where my boss and I got a message one morning that we needed to talk to the boss for an urgent matter. Having no idea what we were walking into, we immediately discovered that the IP address on the computer that we were using in our office for work had been identified as having viewed porn. We locked the office each evening but had allowed our soldiers to take the key and use the computers for morale purposes. This was obviously not the type of morale we had approved. To make matters worse for our porn-viewing soldier, he had not cleared the browsing history, so we were presented with a ready-made list of all the sites that he had visited. The problem that presented itself at that point was that none of us had ever heard of any of the sites—or at least were not comfortable admitting it.

In order to complete the investigation into the egregious violations, we had to confirm the legitimacy of each of the sites that our amateur pornologist had visited. This led us to the only solution we could conceive: we needed to verify each of these websites individually. There were dozens of them, so we cleared our schedules, popped some popcorn, and got special permission to view the sites under the supervision of a military IT specialist. Not surprisingly, we actually had a lot of people offer their help with our efforts. We committed that we would only stay on the sites *just* long enough to confirm that they were valid sites and were in fact pornographic. This, mind you, was a very subjective approach.

Once we completed our inquiry, we were easily able to confirm that some soldier had indeed looked at porn. The problem then became how to prove who it was. The computers had been used by nearly everyone in the unit and we didn't have any technology available to tell us when the sites were visited. After some quasi-serious questioning that yielded no one willing to confess, and although we were fairly certain we knew who the guilty party was, we could not prove anyone's guilt, so we held a formation and doled out some restrictions for the group. No one would be able to use the offices for the next couple of days in the evening, and if it happened again, everyone would be banned going forward.

This was an isolated case, as the pornologist never struck again. The entire situation was more of a molehill than a mountain. It made for a hell of a day and a good story. I got a break for a few hours one day in a hostile combat zone to do something that I would never in a million years ever think possible: I got paid by the US Army to visit pornographic websites. Imagine that on a recruiting poster.

RANGER

THE SECOND ITEM THAT WAS ENJOYABLE, but bordered on violating the rules, was the pet dog that seemingly came to us from nowhere. He was also probably the best thing that happened to my unit during our entire time in Afghanistan. Looking back on it now, I still have no idea how Ranger came to us. I believe the rumor was that one of my soldiers had picked him up from the airfield after his mother had given birth to a litter of puppies. I'm not sure of the truth to this though, as Ranger was the only non-mission related (there were bomb-sniffing and drug-detecting dogs) animal on the base. The only thing I was very certain of was that he had not come from the local community, as he growled and barked at all the local nationals. Although not prohibited specifically by General Order Number 1, maintaining a domesticated animal was against policy, so the day he arrived in the arms of one of my soldiers there was an immediate apprehension. Not having the heart to send him away or the capability to send him somewhere on an airplane, we took a chance on that little puppy and we were rewarded tenfold. Ranger became a confidant and a pseudo-guard dog for my team and brought enrichment to everyone. Before long, he had become an unofficial base mascot and people used to travel to the back side of the base just to see our little guy, many bearing treats that someone had sent them from back home. The veterinary team even started making routine rounds to the ASP, just to check on Ranger and make sure he had a clean bill of health.

Within weeks, Ranger became the worst kept secret on the base and was helping everyone's morale. Some concerns did begin to form over what would happen if he was discovered. I seriously cared nothing for any punishment that would come to me or my team. I was more worried about what would happen to Ranger in the event he were found. I love the Army very much, but we are very rigid in our procedures, and I was terrified that his discovery would lead to his death. All of my concerns were put to rest one morning when I arrived at work. That morning, the commanding general of the 18th Airborne Corps, a three-star general had stopped by and saw our little four-pawed friend as part of his morning run. He too had brought a small treat for the dog. He acknowledged my soldiers but didn't make any statement about the animal, and his lack of action implied acceptance. However, the relief of clearing this large hurdle did come with one large new source of anxiety: frequent visits from the general. As much as I would like to say my work area and my soldiers were inspection-ready at all times, this of course was not the case. Having Ranger was going to make us step up our game.

The relationship with Ranger and the bond we built was deep and as we neared the end of our time overseas, we really started worrying about what would happen to him. While his time with us had been generally accepted on the base, we knew there was no way that we could take him home with us, although I had several soldiers that would have done it in a heartbeat.

In addition, we did not know what the attitude of the unit that was replacing us was on having a unit pet. The type of conversation where you ask someone you've never met to take on caring for an unauthorized pet in a war zone never really comes up via email.

Even if the incoming unit would accept the risk of caring for the dog, there was also a concern with the larger incoming command and its acceptance. As theater's overseas get more mature, strict adherence to the rules becomes more of the norm, so there was significant risk to our furry companion. One of my soldiers mentioned this concern during a visit from the veterinary team. I was pleased when one member of the team immediately responded back with "I'll see what I can do."

That soldier kept his word, and it didn't take long for the wheels to go in motion for Ranger's new home. We were going to turn him over to the veterinary unit, who in turn was going to partner with our mental health medical professionals. Ranger was going to become an emotional support animal to a whole new band of soldiers overseas, much the same way that he had been for us. As our time in the sandy place came close to an end, we began to transition Ranger to his new normal, and he began to split time between us and his new team. As great as it was to leave Afghanistan, it was sad to tell Ranger goodbye, although I know we had done the best that we could for him, much the same as he had done for us.

PART IV: THE STRUGGLES

'Cause I fell on black days
—Soundgarden

THE ACTION

EVEN WITH ALL THE THINGS that I enjoyed and that were good, Afghanistan was wrought with challenges almost daily. While the good stuff is the easiest to recollect, a small scratch of the surface brings a lot of the difficulties back to the forefront. As I sat down to write this book, I laid out my list of topics that I wanted to share and organized them into a table of contents. With each topic that I wrote about, several others would come to mind. Some were consolidated into other stories and some morphed into their own unique chapters. The section that grew the most as I began my writing endeavor is unquestionably this one. The good stuff was the easiest to remember, but the struggles are what left the lasting impact on me. In this silver lining, I learned that these truly are the stories that shaped who I am today—both as a person and as a leader.

I think the best place to start is the combat activity itself. This is the area that everyone wants to ask about, but nearly all are afraid to. Instead, most just go with a customary *how was it?* To answer that general question simply: it was long, it was tiring, and it was scary. The crazy thing about the fear piece was that I had very few instances of hostile activity. I didn't really understand why my experience was relatively peaceful until I uncovered a book written several generations ago.

Carl Von Clausewitz wrote the following in his book, *On War*: "Lastly, even the ultimate outcome of a war is not always to be regarded as final. The defeated state often considers the outcome merely as a transitory evil, for which a remedy may still be found in political conditions at some later date. It is obvious how this, too, can slacken tension and reduce the vigor of the effort."

I don't think the significance of this can be overstated. Although written nearly 200 years ago, this book and excerpt provide a clear view of modern day conflict and explain long-protracted war. Clausewitz argued that only through absolute war (basically pure destruction) could you defeat an enemy. His writings were based off the military theories that Napoleon executed during his conflicts. Clausewitz believed that one must take away the will of their enemy to fight back. Efforts to effectively win must be lasting and it must be impressionable, otherwise the enemy and conflict will repeat itself. World War II does not meet the technical definition of absolute war, but it's the closest that we have seen in the last several generations. The toll of the conflict with the sheer loss of life in Germany from a two-front war and the impact of two atomic bombs on Japan served to provide nearly the same end state. The US has been involved in multiple conflicts in the last seventy-plus years since then, but none have been near the magnitude of World War II. Basically every conflict since then has simply lingered.

When the US started bombing and subsequently invaded Afghanistan after 9/11, we toppled and overthrew the Taliban regime with a lot of ease. They continued to have some strongholds in remote areas, but for the most part, my time in Afghanistan occurred during the transition period discussed in Clausewitz's work.

I didn't realize this while I served, and don't get me wrong, it doesn't mean that everything was all unicorns and rainbows. I remember one of my first walks through the ASP a day or two after arriving, where we found a fresh trip wire on our perimeter attached to a land mine. At the time, this was most likely the most terrifying thing that I had ever experienced in my life, but in the grand scheme of things, it served to help raise my awareness about my new surroundings. I have described some situations previously of uncomfortable circumstances that I found myself in, but for the most part I think I could count the aggressive actions of the enemy on one hand. My workplace gave me three of those incidents. The first was the land mine that I just mentioned and the second was the discovery of another threat. I have mentioned several times the amount of land mines there were on the base and the efforts to clear those mines. In this particular situation, we were clearing mines to expand our base perimeter and grow my ASP. There was an old Russian bathhouse a little bit outside our current concertina wire fence that we had considered using as a new field office. I received a report that the mine sweeping team had completed their duties and that the bathhouse was clear. We were able to start planning our expansion. The next day after clearing was complete, the Marine Corps gunnery sergeant and I headed out to check out the building and were alarmed to find a cache of rocket-propelled grenades (RPGs) staged for a potential attack on the base. There were probably twenty of them and all I could think of was the magnitude of *what if we had waited?* These RPGs were snuck into this building, less than a hundred yards from our current boundary. From there, any shot could have impacted any location on base. It was a stark reminder of where I was.

The last incident from the ASP was probably the most dramatic of my time there. I was awakened one night by a report that the ASP was under attack and that our quick reaction force had responded. An emergency resupply of over 3,000 rounds of ammunition was required and we were trying to put together the pieces. Whatever had happened led the perimeter guard force to call for support and the response was so robust that my internal guards had to hunker down behind barricades in order to not get shot. I even heard rumors of pilots on the runway lying on the ground with visible tracer rounds flying overhead. The unofficial story was that apparently three men on horseback had popped a few shots at the guard towers, but that was never confirmed. Three thousand plus rounds later there were no dead bodies that could be found and by the next morning, there was no official story. It wasn't mentioned in any base force protection briefings. It was like the whole thing never happened.

The only other hostile incident worth mentioning during my time in Afghanistan was the night of the rocket attack. It was *the* rocket attack because it was the only one that impacted us during our entire time in country. This event should probably have been viewed as more significant as it hit so close that it actually shook people out of bed, but the weapon systems and ability to aim of that insurgency were so poor that we actually felt pretty sure that they wouldn't be able to get that close again. That was the best shot they had and all they generated were a bunch of service members running out in their pajamas wearing body armor. Once we all realized what was going on, fear was replaced by bad jokes. We waited about fifteen minutes until the all-clear was given and headed to bed. That was the one and only time I had to get in the bunkers for a legitimate reason that wasn't a drill.

Things in Afghanistan were poor before I arrived and got really nasty after I left. I thank God that I arrived during the transitory period between the original conflict and the introduction of the insurgency that brought with it snipers and roadside bombs. It sounds crazy to say, but I got lucky to be there so early.

LIVING BESIDE A RUNWAY

SUPPORTING THIS OPERATION early on was good as far as not getting shot at, but bad as far as the living accommodations. Hot, cold, dirty, and cramped almost became a state of mind, and I had committed myself to soldiering on. I did leave out a couple painful items about my living arrangements that I want to get into now.

I have found myself far too frequently watching those completely staged, *I need a house* shows on television in recent years (yes, there was nothing else on). I love the complaints of those that are too noisy because they are too close to highways or railroad crossings. While I do agree that I have no desire to leave near one of those myself, I can't help but remember my time living right beside a military airfield. As I previously wrote, Bagram Airfield had just over a six-mile-loop on the base, with the airfield in the middle. The ASP that I worked at was on one side of the base, and my tent was on the other. I pretty much had a vantage point at all times for every plane coming and going—sometimes by sight but always by sound.

Military cargo planes can be loud up close, but over time their sounds became innocuous and I barely noticed them. Jets on the other hand, were a totally different story. When I first arrived in country, the predominant fighter jet in service was the A-10

Thunderbolt, which was affectionately nicknamed the *Warthog*. This plane's primary mission was close air support to ground forces and the sole function of the Air Force contingency that worked out of our ASP was to supply these aircraft. Like the cargo planes, these jets were significantly louder, but I got used to them after a short period.

My ability to basically ignore the air mission changed pretty drastically with the arrival of the Marine Corps Harriers. My relationship with these jets started with infatuation, with their ability to launch and land vertically without a runway. Holy shit was it loud, though. During the workday, I could live with this noise, but most of our fighting operations occurred at night. The sound of these planes taking off could have brought a dead person back to life. Getting to sleep in my tent was hard enough with large temperatures swings and the noises and smells that come with having eight roommates. Being awakened in the middle of the night most times then led to some form of insomnia. It sucked, but I always told myself that if the Harriers deployed, we were kicking ass and winning, so my sleep was a small sacrifice to make.

The lack of sleep and fascination with the different jets that made their way to the base were all basically just an appetizer for the F14s that deployed. They were not American-owned and for the life of me, I can't remember which country was flying them. All I know is that they created one of the hairiest issues during my entire deployment. Our runway wasn't very long on the airfield and each plane took nearly every inch of available space to both take off and land. For this incident, I believe it was a foggy morning and the pilot misjudged the runway and landed his aircraft too late, not leaving enough space to stop. I am not sure if the pilot was exceptionally brave or stupid, as he never ejected from the fighter jet. He barreled off the end of the runway and brought the plan to a stop in the middle of an active minefield. To the left of where his aircraft rested was the base fuel farm that housed hundreds of thousands of gallons of jet fuel and to his right was the bomb storage in the ASP. Compounding these issues in his surroundings was the fact that his plane was carrying both fuel pods and bombs. Someway, somehow, with maybe some divine intervention and a lot of luck, he did not strike a land mine as he was bringing this jet to a stop. Simply put, this could have been absolutely catastrophic.

This event caused us to evacuate nearly one-third of the base. In fact, I didn't let most of my soldiers go to work for a few days, and we left a skeleton guard crew on site that handled any emergency ammunition issues. The plane rescue effort was amazing, with the Polish team clearing mines, followed by the Air Force removal of the bombs and fuel pods. Finally, a crane was deployed to lift the fighter jet out of its landing spot. It was a total team effort that could have gone wrong at so many points, but it didn't. This is one of many things that went, *just right* for me while I was overseas.

THE VILLAGE

THREADING A NEEDLE to avoid a catastrophe seemed to be a consistent theme for my team. Before I get into another wild story about that, I would be remiss not to mention the other trying portion of the geographic location of my canvas palace: the village that sat just outside our perimeter. I just discussed the impact of the airfield on my sleep, but it barely held a candle to the loudspeakers broadcasting prayers each morning. First light in Islam brings about the first prayer and, to an unsuspecting soldier, a blaring Farsi message that was louder than any rooster crow. It only lasted a few minutes each morning, but I liken it to some form of institutional torture that I firmly believe got louder each day. I got up and went to work every morning in country with no days off because there was no point trying to sleep in.

Even with that, surveying my twenty-two years in the service, far and away my best experiences occurred when I was in Afghanistan as a young lieutenant. Some of the things that made Afghanistan stand out to me mainly involved the people, including both the local nationals and my fellow services. This same village just outside the wall provided me with a lot of great interactions, stressful workdays, and one of the scariest experiences of my life. It didn't start out that way. Our efforts in the village seemed really simple when we first got the mission from our battalion. We were to go out into the local community and pick up concrete jersey barricades and overhead bunkers that were shaped like Cs. The local villagers were creating them for us and all told we had to fetch several hundred of each.

The artisanship of these local masons was a sight to see. Watching them craft these barriers, it felt like I had stepped out of a time machine in the past. There was no concrete plant, nor mixers or pump trucks. There wasn't a Home Depot, Lowe's, or Menards to buy bags of concrete to start from. Every ounce of concrete that went into these barriers was homemade from centuries-old recipes that had been passed down through many generations. They used no exact measurements or ratios. I am not going to lie, there was some concern upfront about the integrity of their construction methods, but after looking at the structures that were still standing in this war torn country, a little peace of mind was at least partially realized.

The village was considered friendly and we had the support of the local community because we were paying handsomely for these concrete force protection devices. The first time I sent my soldiers out I didn't go with them, thinking nothing of the job. That all changed two hours later when they returned to base telling stories of being robbed blind. Everything they carried outside the wire had been stolen. The local children had pilfered straps, dunnage, water cans, and fuel cans. I would say everything that wasn't tied down was taken, but that would be inaccurate, because they cut things off the trucks as well. The decision was made to abandon the mission on that first day, but we would have to go back the following week, as the base was at a severe force protection risk without any adequate overhead cover. Looking back now, the plan and decisions we made as a unit to complete this assignment were nothing short of stupid. Over half the citizens in the local community were still armed, and in order to remain light, the decision was made to have the trucks go out into the village escorted only by a forklift. The soldiers riding shotgun, including myself, would exit the vehicles in the village and we would just burn and turn trucks from the village to inside the base to drop off cargo and back out to the village to get more. What this meant was that basically myself, four soldiers, and a guy in a forklift were sitting ducks, standing in the middle of this village off post with only one radio. We had no means of transportation other than the forklift that could run about seven miles an hour and didn't have enough space to transport us anyway. If anything were to go south, this could have easily been calamitous. The first time we went out with this configuration things went well and we continued to do this week after week. This is another time to stress that we weren't very intelligent, as we started doing this every Monday, which was against force protection guidance to not do things consistently. That part never actually bit us in the ass. After that first poor morning, everything went really well for us in that village—until it didn't. The elders had kept the children in line for the most part and we completed this tasking with very little fanfare. On the morning of our harrowing experience, we were out in the village on what seemed like a normal Monday towards the end of the mission, except for the fact that the kids were a little rowdier this day. They were actually diving in front of our trucks and when we would stop someone would climb on the back of the truck to steal the little bit of dunnage that we brought (at this point, it was only straps and wood). Things were starting to escalate quickly and we were struggling to control the movement of the children. The elders helped a little, but it was a chaotic scene. In the process of doing a quick turnaround, while trying to avoid striking one of the kids in our very large, palletized loading trucks, one of my soldiers accidentally ran over what amounted to two sticks stuck in the ground with a crossbar spanning across them. I had never noticed this item before. It turns out that this was one of the rudimentary soccer goals for this local village team. Any power that we possessed evaporated in that moment. In the distance, I saw a group of well-dressed young men all decked out in brand new soccer attire marching towards the field. Apparently, this was the warlord's sponsored soccer team and they had a game that day. We had destroyed one of their goals and I had exactly zero trucks in the vicinity to get our asses out of there. As I was piecing this all together, a near riot formed with several hundred people around us. To say that I was terrified wouldn't even do that word justice.

What I can describe next is nothing short of being touched by an angel. A young woman emerged from the crowd who was able to speak English, and she began to negotiate for us. Apparently, she was a westerner who was there to teach English. The enormity of this young woman's mission in country was awe-inspiring. Afghanistan, at this time, was still recovering from the oppressive Taliban regime and its harsh policies toward women. Even in late 2002, young girls still could not attend school. In the beginning of her intervention, she was exceptionally terse with us and me in particular. I felt as if she was chastising us, but was fine with it because she also calmed the crowd down. As our trucks started arriving back in the village, I held each of them until we had enough transport to get everyone out. We also began the process of using our dunnage straps to secure the goal together temporarily. With our provisional repair in place, I promised to return another day with a new soccer goal. She was skeptical of my commitment, but nevertheless helped us secure safe passage out of the village. We kept our pledge to the village and had a soccer goal made, delivering it on our next trip outside the perimeter. As far as our angel is concerned, I never got her name and I never saw her again, but in my heart, I grasped the truth that she saved our lives that day. I don't know if she was a real person or simply a real angel that came to save us, but I will never forget that day.

CHICKEN STREET

THE LAST STORY that I have about barely escaping a debacle centered around one of the quid pro quos that I mentioned earlier, involved a holiday shopping trip and the base provost marshal. A gun and ammunition are not normal accessories for a holiday shopping trip, except maybe in Texas, but these, including body armor, were necessary accompaniments, for the most memorable shopping expedition of my life. I had previously been out into the economy in Kabul to purchase some items for the base as was standard during my early days in Afghanistan, but on this random day I found myself feeling rich, with a pocketful of money heading into town to make some Christmas purchases. The ridiculousness of putting myself in harms way to purchase items that no one really needed may not have been my brightest moment, but in those days, I was craving a break. We loaded up in two midsize SUVs with four service members each. Each person was in full body armor and tactical helmet, with loaded weapons and enough extra munitions to fight off a small army. The drive itself was completely uneventful, and before long we found ourselves in downtown Kabul struggling to find two parking spaces next to each other near the world-famous market street. To put finding a parking space into context, we were trying to find a place to park as close to the market as possible, but the scene resembled the French Quarter during Mardi Gras. We weren't fighting other cars for parking as much as we were navigating around people.

Finally, we found two spots near each other and we quickly parked. As we got out of our vehicles, we were greeted by a large man who ask us for money to clean our windows. He was the largest local that I had ever laid eyes on. He had no cleaner, or wipes, or squeegee, and I was fairly certain that he had no intention of cleaning anything. As I was about to open my mouth in protest, one of the gentlemen with me pulled out a crisp $20 bill to pay him. It turns out we were paying for vehicle protection, not cleaning, and our vehicles would now be safe for our time spent in the city. At this point, we broke off in teams to explore the markets and to find just the right thing to send home that our loved ones probably didn't need. The scene that unfolded in front of me is difficult to describe. It was just a sea of people. It was loud, chaotic, and busy. The only two things I could liken it to are scenes that you may see on National Geographic TV or Black Friday at Walmart, where a thousand people are fighting over seven discounted televisions. For me, it was both scary and exhilarating.

Popular items for us to shop for included jewelry, muskets, rugs, and bootleg DVDs. Haggling and bartering was fun but exhausting, and before long it was time to meet up with all the other soldiers to head home for the evening. It had been a good day, a break from the norm that was soon to shift to one of stress and terror. I'm not exactly sure how it happened, but as one of my soldiers attempted to unlock the SUV door that he was driving, he somehow broke the key off into the lock. We had no spare with us and the base was nearly a forty-five minute drive away. The sun was starting to set and we had but two options: we could load everyone up in one vehicle and haul-ass back to base knowing that the vehicle would be left overnight and therefore would not be there in the morning, or we could try to pull a rabbit out of our hat.

We made the decision to stick around and to try to fix the problem because no one wanted to explain to the boss that his vehicle was gone forever. Additionally, the paperwork involved and investigation would have been excruciating, and that most likely would have been everyone's last trip into town. Luckily, one member of our team that had traveled to Kabul with us was a translator for the provost marshal. He began to engage our mountain of a vehicle guard. Less than ten minutes later, a local locksmith appeared. He expeditiously moved to take the lock assembly out of the vehicle. He instructed us that he would be back in less than an hour and was confident he could fix our problem.

The next sixty minutes were nearly the longest of my life. We were effectively sitting ducks in the middle of this crowded city and could have been susceptible to any form of attack. Additionally there was a risk trusting the intentions of this locksmith. If he could fix the key, all he would have to do was wait us out until night fall when we would have to leave. He could have swept in and taken the vehicle for himself at this point. We were holding out hope that he would be back and began to pool the remaining money we had leftover to make sure we could pay him. He could have charged us any amount of money and we would have gladly paid him anything we had left to our names.

In just under an hour, with the sun setting, our savior arrived back at our vehicle with the key in hand, soldered back together. He reinstalled the lock assembly and handed us the key. For his troubles, he wanted a whopping twenty-five dollars. We paid him his full asking price and even threw in a tip. I know for myself personally, I said a small prayer of thanks under my breath. We loaded up and headed back to base, relieved that our potential nightmare was over. As we communicated the story to our commander, I was chastised a little for worrying about losing the vehicle. The safety of the soldiers was much more important, I was told.

Ironically, about a week later, another group of anxious shoppers were heading to Kabul to fulfill their holiday wishes when a local attempted to throw an explosive device into their vehicle. This effectively ended all unnecessary shopping trips from that point forward. I was just happy the soldiers were okay and honestly didn't care that the shopping trips were over. The heaviness of that incident hit me hard and I knew just how lucky I was. I had been there, done that, had a musket, a rug, and one hell of a story to tell.

ANIMAL THUNDERDOME

THERE IS ONE MORE GROUP of local inhabitants that impacted my time in Afghanistan. The Middle East offers many challenges, among them frightening and annoying wildlife. My first trip to that part of the world was to Egypt, where there was an abundance of scorpions. They were so prevalent that we were told to cover the top of or boots with socks each night so they would not crawl in and to be wary of where we put our feet down in the mornings. They were venomous and scary but not very mobile, so many bored soldiers found sport in trying to catch them. I believe the worst thing I ever witnessed was *Scorpion Battledome*, where there were several soldiers gathered around a vehicle drip pan watching two scorpions fight. I don't know that their original intent was scorpion fighting, but apparently putting two scorpions in a confined space together led to an entertaining contest.

The scene in Afghanistan was much different. I don't believe I saw a scorpion the entire time I was in country, but I was constantly bombarded by rats. They were everywhere. Normal rats in the United States move in the shadows to meet their objective to get food. Middle Eastern rats do everything short of pulling up a chair to join you at the dinner table. They were so prevalent that it wasn't uncommon to see a random water bottle go flying across our break tent to hit one that was trying to get into our stash of MREs. While this was annoying, for the most part they were harmless, and after a time, I became immune to the sight of them. Actually, I became numb to all wildlife over there until the day I encountered my first snake, which led to one of the most petrifying experiences of my entire deployment.

I hate snakes! is a sentiment shared by me and one of the greatest explorers off all time, Indiana Jones. Well actually, my top three animal fears as a youngster were snakes, alligators, and sharks. Growing up in West Virginia, I'm not sure of the rationale for the latter two (I didn't go to Florida for the first time until I was eighteen), but I do know my fear of snakes was real. I can still remember playing in my grandmother's backyard when I was little when a snake came slithering out from a piece of wood and traversed through my legs unbothered. Although it did me no harm, I found out later it was a copperhead (one of the two venomous snakes in the region) and that cemented my fear further. Once during my teen years, a friend and I were doing yard work for a local business when I uncovered a snake. The sight of the snake startled me and I am elated that my friend could not hear the shrill scream that I let out. My friend's car was parked nearby, and I grabbed the only tool that I could find to kill it—a golf club. My first fear-laden swing missed the snake entirely, which is damned embarrassing because at the time, I was a baseball player and had no issue hitting an 80mph fastball. After another failed attempt to kill this beast, and with my best friend laying on the ground laughing at me, I finally got enough wits about me to kill the snake and struck it enough times to kill it several times over. I moved it into the road and continued working. But every time the snake caught my eye, still flailing on the ground despite its detached head, it caused my heart to skip a beat.

Fast forward back to Afghanistan, where I had my first Middle Eastern snake encounter. When I arrived in country, they were building two large tent developments for the projected future base population. One of the tent cities we were building was nicknamed *Viper* because they had cleared so many from the tent site in order for construction to begin. I can't remember the name of the tent city I lived in, but for this reason, Viper always stuck out to me. I had not physically seen a snake in country for my first couple of months until one fateful day. I was working at our ASP when one of my sergeants yelled into our office trailer for me to come check something out. I didn't really know what to expect, but I obliged the request. As I walked out the door and started down the steps, I observed an ammunition box laying on the ground several feet in front of me and my sergeant holding a stick. He opened up the box immediately and out slithered, you guessed it, a king cobra. Holy shit, I was paralyzed. I mean you can't make this stupid shit up. The sergeant quickly placed his stick on the back of the snake, which would not allow it any movement. This pissed the snake off and caused it to bow-up with its head fully erect. I felt as if I was looking eye to eye with this venomous slithering fiend. There was no antivenom on base, so I knew that one bite would most likely be a death sentence. The sergeant, who clearly considered himself some kind of junior Crocodile Hunter yelled out, "Don't worry, I milked the venom," but I couldn't have cared less. I wasn't putting my faith in this ridiculous amateur snake handler. At this moment, I felt like I had been demoted from the top of the food chain and I screamed multiple obscenities with the central theme of *put the damn snake up you dumb SOB and get rid of it*. My sergeant obliged my request and forced the snake back into the box and then ask me how to get rid of it. This reply troubled me greatly, as it further stressed how shortsighted he was, catching one of the most dangerous animals in the world with no escape plan. I suggested he burn the box when he sternly informed me that we had to have the dunnage from the box from an accountability standpoint. This scenario quickly rolled through my mind as I imagined my explanation to my boss that someone died because we were worried about accounting for a wooden box. I didn't want to leave his vehicle overnight on a market street but telling him I burned a wooden box seemed pretty benevolent. At this point, I offered to write a memo for the write-off; this solution didn't seem too difficult to me. From there, I'm not sure exactly what my sergeant did with the snake, but about an hour later it was gone and we never talked about it again, nor did I ever write the memo. I did see the snake a few more times in my dreams while I was there, but luckily never encountered one again. In a master of the obvious moment, sponsored by the Army, I did put out guidance at our next unit gathering that no one was allowed to catch and keep snakes or any other wildlife. It seems crazy to have to explain this, kind of like the caution label on a hot coffee cup, but sometimes being overseas can make you a little bit crazy.

YOUNG LEADERS

AT THIS POINT, I want to switch gears to the mental toll that this deployment took on me. Nearly eighteen years removed from our efforts, I still vividly remember the stresses that I felt and just how difficult it was. I have been working in the civilian world about fifteen years now and I have heard repeatedly that the hardest job in any organization is that of the frontline leader. In some instances I would agree with this assessment, but in many I feel that this wasn't the case. In comparing the civilian world to the military, I can easily argue that there is not an assignment in any civilian organization that comes anywhere near the difficulty of being a frontline leader in the United States military, particularly in a hostile theater. I am not saying this in any way to bolster myself. It's just the truth. The military, by its nature, is incredibly arduous on both the body and, more importantly, the mind. Men and women every day meet the same challenges as I did and the resilience that they display is unparalleled and frankly astonishing.

The difficulty of these assignments can't be overstated for a variety of reasons. For starters, many soldiers, officer and enlisted alike, are exceptionally young and have not reached full maturity, but they must display pristine emotional intelligence. Two of the most visible leaders in every platoon are the young sergeants who are just experiencing their first leadership assignments after serving a few years and the newly minted lieutenants, who are usually in their first assignment after college. These leaders are generally in their early twenties, and no matter the struggle or harshness encountered, they must lead, as they are who our fighters follow. Whether or not they believe in the mission or their orders (it's important to note that this is a selfish age group), they must execute their orders without question or cracking in front of those that they must guide. Without these leaders being in lockstep with the commander's intent, failures can result, ranging from single actions up to potentially the entire mission.

Second, in many situations, these leaders must act contrary to their natural instinct of survival. We are going to haul this, escort that, storm over there, or sometimes just simply fight. They must put the mission first, which by its nature will place them in harm's way. They cannot waiver, they cannot crack, and must be a pillar that is rigid in any storm. As these chiefs go, so goes their subordinates. To piggyback on my story from earlier, I didn't go out to the village on our first assignment, but as soon as there was an issue, my soldiers never set foot in that community again without me.

Third, these leaders must put the needs of their service members above their own. They are in meetings while their subordinates are waiting in line for the phones. They are planning the next day's activities while others are sleeping. They are the last to get hot food when it is served in the field or the guy stuck with the tuna noodle casserole MRE when someone else gets the chili mac. Their sacrifice is thankless and hard and damn, it's tough. They get less and the ass end of everything.

Lastly, and the most important reason why the jobs of these leaders are so demanding and their efforts so astonishing is the fact that they are human, and therefore imperfect. They miss home, major events, and family. They experience tragedy the same as those that serve under them, but they still have to lead and make hard decisions. The leaders don't get to take days off when they get bad news or a relationship ends. They must balance compassion with the military's needs and make decisions that are often unpopular.

I mentioned the term *resilience* earlier, which later in the Global War on Terror became a military buzzword. There was a lot of energy, money and effort put into teaching it, and while all that is helpful, nothing galvanizes you like that first *oh shit* moment where you just have to figure it out. And you carry this with you. I know that I have sometimes upset those around me (my wife in particular) by my lack of outrage or emotion when someone does not act the way I feel they should. I may be angry and upset deep in my heart, but in my mind, I am plotting my path to just deal with it. That is probably one of the greatest strengths of these young leaders—an innate desire to solve problems and fix bad situations.

To further emphasize my point about the difficult yet critical role of these leaders, I want to refer back to Clausewitz one more time, who stated that "War is a continuation of policy by other means." Whether the conflict is wildly popular (First Gulf War, Operation Enduring Freedom) or one that begins with great fanfare and sours quickly (Vietnam, Second Iraq War), these young leaders must remain committed to their duty, regardless of which side of history they might land on. They fight for their flag, their country, and their subordinates, and obey their orders.

I would also be remiss not to also touch on the fact that the American military has at times been a social justice experiment, which has further strained these leaders. About a year ago, there was a large scale debate over the transgender ban in the military. I originally did not plan to write this here, but once I did, I couldn't bring myself to delete it. I also want to clarify that I have no issue whatsoever with those that undergo this life change, I just have concerns as it relates to military service. In no way do I ever want to politicize my service, but I remember seeing a gentleman being interviewed on TV who basically said that the leaders in the military should just have to deal with transgender service members. I call bullshit. While the military is probably the closest thing to a diverse utopia in the United States, asking these young leaders to tackle this scorching hot button issue is too much. There are standards, rules, and regulations in place not to ensure that the military is a diverse democracy, but to attempt to make us closer to a meritocracy. Everyone in the military falls under the same set of rules. There are some exceptions to this, but my point is simple. The military by its nature is a bit of a petri dish, but there are some specimens that do not make it into the sample. I'm not saying there is anything wrong with those individuals who don't, for whatever reason meet its requirements (too tall, too short, too fat, too thin, too young, too old, various mental or physical medical conditions, etc.). I am simply stating that sometimes we don't want to introduce outside factors that could severely disrupt that ecosystem without a well-thought-out plan, particularly when it serves such a vital function as national defense.

To illustrate my point further, President Truman issued Executive Order 9981 in 1948 to end segregation in the military. As simple as this sounds, this transition still took nearly six years to integrate the last regiment. Even still it was nearly another ten years before Defense Directive 5120.36, which pushed for the elimination of discrimination against black troops outside of the military bases. It was nearly fifteen years from executive order until the mission was complete. Simply giving an order doesn't change the dynamic of the day to day actions. It may make news headlines and be celebrated publicly, but privately it's hell and these young leaders are the ones that must execute. I have lauded the efforts of these young men and women and if anyone could deal with this sudden change, it's them. I am just saying, they shouldn't have to. We owe them a better plan.

THE HEARTBROKEN, THE CHIEF, AND A FEMALE SOLDIER

TRANSITIONING FROM THE NEAR-DEATH EXPERIENCES and to caveat off the mental challenges of being a leader, I wanted to touch briefly on just how exacting it is to be on stage every day as a leader. I had many great interactions with my soldiers, but I can assure you that most became a challenge from time to time, typically just briefly. I did have a few whose issues just seemed to linger and I wanted to share them here.

Absence makes the heart grow fonder is an old proverb that came from a 1650 work where writer James Howell observed that "distance sometimes endears friendship and absence sweeteneth it." I had heard the expression many times before and due to the shortness of most of my previous trips away (usually three months or less without seeing someone), I had never seen it put to the test. As I have already mentioned, Afghanistan had poor phone connections and very few internet options, which meant that soldiers would truly be absent from their loved ones for long periods of time. What I learned watching this proverb being put through the wringer was that the expression was only half true. If the heart was really fond before one departed, in many situations the affection did grow while they were away. The largest contributing factor was the appreciation that was gained for others. In contrast though, if there were some cracks in a relationship, distance wasn't going to fix it. In fact, it would turn a crack into a crater.

As I just mentioned when discussing being a young leader, I got really good at compartmentalizing my feelings. I had a relationship come to an end while I was deployed, which was my doing, as I wanted to focus on Afghanistan and I didn't think I was being fair to her. I also had a family member die that I learned about on one of my brief phone calls. I had to take both of these in stride, and I would be shocked if my soldiers ever knew that anything was weighing on me. The same cannot be said for many of my soldiers, several of which saw their love fall to pieces. As the leader in charge, it was my job to continue to get them to provide their best effort every day, even when all they wanted to do was stay in bed mourning. I remember one soldier in particular whose marriage fell apart. I had spoken to him many times about his home situation and he stayed positive while everyone around him watched the train wreck in progress. It started with photos she sent where she obviously looked as if she was either drunk or high. He just brushed those photos off. All he could see was that she was smiling, which made him happy since he knew how upset she had been. He was the missing the proverbial forest for the trees. One day he declared he had *good news* that he wanted to share with anyone who would listen. One of his friends was going to start staying at his house to help out his wife, as she was struggling with the deployment. He thought his friend was being a good guy for helping her out. He told me and all of his peers that this was best, but we feared the worse. He continued to lie to himself all the way up until the day she picked him up at the airport when we got home. She never took him home, though. They stopped at a hotel along the way where she informed him their marriage was over. He was shattered. I felt bad that it was held over his head for so long and he struggled with it every day. Deep down, I think he knew how it was going to end, but he couldn't face that reality. He needed something to hold onto.

This was one example, but I am fairly sure that every one of my soldiers had at least a few bad days because of life at home, which didn't stop while we were away. Being in an atmosphere where filters were already reduced, the rawness of these emotions were always a struggle to contain and deal with. The easy answer would have been to punish anyone who acted out, but that wouldn't solve the problem and wouldn't have helped the soldier, either. One of the hardest parts of the entire situation was acting with compassion, even when challenged. But we needed each other. Our country needed those soldiers, the soldiers needed support at home and good leaders in theater, and I needed everybody.

A heartbroken soldier is tough to handle, but I always understood the root cause of their actions. The same cannot be said for the stubborn ones who in many cases were as hard-headed as their lieutenant. There was one soldier in particular who fit this description. The structure of the ASP staff was slightly different than a lot of units. I had a warrant officer assigned to me to serve as the accountable officer for the ammunition property that we stored. I was in charge of the overall facility, while the chief was in charge of the inventory. This dichotomy was the origin of our friction and caused us to rub each other the wrong way for several months.

For those that are not familiar with the military rank of warrant officers, they are a group that are basically treated like gods, being senior enlisted soldiers that are commissioned as officers because of their technical expertise. They are affectionately called *Chiefs*. Their opinions are rarely challenged, and although technically even the most senior warrant officer is still a lower rank than the lowest lieutenant, one would be hard pressed to find a warrant officer that actually believes this. Now, this isn't to trash the Army Warrant Officer Corps, as I have worked with some phenomenal chiefs, but as with every group, there are a few bad apples that get lobbed in with the rest. My chief in Afghanistan wasn't a bad apple; I just think he was a little sour. To be fair, I was sour too. Our combination was anything but sweet.

The relationship started very tame. At Fort Lewis, we actually spent a ton of time together. We golfed, bowled, played cards, and were part of the same group that spent many weekends together as geographical bachelors. The rub started nearly the moment we got to Afghanistan together after we assumed responsibility for our mission. Chief started his power play early, and it instantly took us off of good footing. The tension started over something as simple as the access roster to the ASP. Being the accountable officer, Chief was responsible for determining levels of access. He did grant me full unescorted access to the facility but set my commander's access as *escort required*. This sent Captain Pope through the roof and I honestly couldn't blame him since technically he was the command authority that signed the memo. Picture a scenario in the civilian world where the guy who approves all the access to a building is not actually allowed to be inside without an escort. It was maddening and stupid.

This is how things started and they pretty much proceeded off the cliff from there. I believed our job in Afghanistan was to be customer-centric and to find a way to help the war fighter. Chief, on the other hand, was very process-driven and didn't want to waiver and make exceptions. If someone showed up with improperly filled out paperwork, Chief was more than happy to send them away, even if that happened more than once. This was asinine to me. In many situations, these soldiers were driving to us from other bases and putting their lives in jeopardy. No way in hell would I turn them away because their paperwork was wrong. I got to the point where I started doing quality control on all our customer's documents before they got to Chief. If there was a way to get them ammunition, we were going to do it. My behavior infuriated Chief, but I was tired of arguing with him about process and customer service so I just eliminated the conflict point—but I guess I created another.

The biggest blowup that we partook in nearly got him fired and fractured the unit almost to the point of no return. We had been tasked to support the State Department and their efforts in Kabul training the Afghan National Army. This was our highest profile mission to date and we had been told repeatedly to give them whatever they wanted. That memo made it to Chief and he was fully supportive in the beginning, until the State Department changed their request multiple times. I could understand his frustration but saying no just wasn't an option for us. Chief didn't feel this way. In fact, after about the fourth change he declared that it was his ammunition and the State Department would get what he saw fit. We had previously kept the tension between us away from my soldiers up to this point, but on this day in particular it all boiled over and there was no containment. We yelled and screamed at each other in the middle of the ASP so loud that I think local villagers could hear us. It got so heated at one point that I gave him a direct order and dared him to violate it. The confrontation never got anywhere near physical, but the unit commander had to separate us. I was fuming after this situation, but after I calmed down, I was embarrassed. I blamed Chief for the origin of the confrontation but blamed myself for the escalation. I knew better.

After this incident, more out of necessity than desire, Chief and I figured out how to tolerate each other to finish the mission and the State Department got everything that it needed (and then some). By the end of the deployment, we were bordering on cordial. I even remember Chief saying as we were departing that he looked forward to working together again. I said the same back to him, knowing that we were both lying.

As bad as the first two types of soldiers were to deal with, nothing compares to the third type of challenging soldier, the *perpetual problem soldier*. This soldier follows the 80/20 rule of Pareto's Law, where as a leader 80 percent of your problems (and time) derive from 20 percent of your people. Every organization (and statistical model) falls into this simple rule, so it is natural to expect it in the Army as well. This soldier (employee) provides consistent issues daily while tiptoeing near the line that they know they can't cross. My most memorable problem soldier from Afghanistan was a specialist assigned to the unit. This soldier also just happened to be a female that was both young and attractive. Being a young male, this compounded any problem I had with her.

I had met and interacted with everyone in the unit within my first few days of being assigned there but had very few in-depth conversations. My first real conversation with this specialist occurred at the aforementioned Holidome bar. It was after a long day at work and I was sitting at the bar, eating dinner, and enjoying a cold adult beverage. The specialist approached me and sat down, and over the course of the next several minutes we had a very cordial conversation. I found the conversation to be innocuous and before long she went on her way. I was immediately approached by several male soldiers in the unit who told me to watch out for her and that she was no good. I assured them that I would give her the benefit of the doubt and that I wasn't looking for a fraternizing relationship. Plus she had just informed me that she was engaged to another soldier in the unit.

After my initial conversation with the specialist, the next few months provided to be rather uneventful. All that changed when the unit went to the field. This was the training exercise where I was away from the unit and on one of the rare opportunities that I got to see my team, I received a complaint that someone had called the specialist a whore. Because this was eighteen years ago (prior to the Me Too Movement), I was not instantly outraged. Instead, I asked for context. As it turns out, the specialist's fiancée was working on the ROTC mission and did not go to the field, but several of his friends did. As the story progressed, I found out that one of his friends walked into a tent and witnessed the specialist giving a back and shoulder rub to another male soldier who was shirtless. I understood the issue and tried my best to smooth everything over as I had no desire to punish the soldier. I did make him apologize to the specialist for what he said.

Over the next several weeks, the relationship between the
specialist and this new male soldier continued to blossom, and
before long, her engagement was over. I found out that this
relationship began in earnest after the two soldiers had gone to a
class together to learn how to use our ammunition management
software. Many of the soldiers in the unit were not happy about
this new relationship, but that faded with time. As we went through
medical processing, a small issue was found with my specialist and
I was given the option whether to allow her to deploy or not. She
begged me for the opportunity to serve her country, and against my
better judgement, I said yes. The rest of the mobilization was going
well until we got overseas, where it progressed to fall off the rails
quickly. My two lovebirds were assigned to be our ASP computer
administrators along with another soldier, but due to their consistent
flirting and slacking off, the determination was made that they had
to be separated. Because the love interest was much better than my
specialist at operating the software platform, she was moved out of
the office to work in the ASP.

At around the same time, we received a tasking as a unit to run
the base wash rack (a large car wash). This job was quite easy. All
our soldier had to do was to keep the generators and pumps filled
with fuel, schedule units to come to the wash rack to clean their
equipment and to mitigate any conflicts, and make sure that the
units cleaned up after themselves. The only physical labor required
was the actual filling of fuel cans and equipment. Our plan was to
staff this on a rotation and we chose to send the specialist there first.
She was infuriated and felt this job was beneath her. Her first ploy
to get out of this duty was to go to sick call and complain about the
medical condition that should have kept her from going overseas in
the first place. She returned with a physical limitation profile that she
could not lift more than twenty-five pounds. In her mind, the five-
gallon fuel cans, when full, weighed more than twenty-five pounds,
so obviously she couldn't work there anymore. You can imagine the

look on her face when she was told to just fill the cans half full and make two trips. I didn't make her do that to be an ass; it was to prove a point to our soldiers that they didn't control the narrative. Not surprisingly, she headed back to the medical tent the next morning and returned with another physical profile that stated that she could only work in an office area. She handed me this dirty piece of paper with a smile on her face that reached from ear to ear. I made a beeline straight to the medical tent and blew through the doors. As I held the piece of paper up, the first person I encountered just pointed at someone else and quickly stated "I wanted nothing to do with that." Once I found the target of my frustration, I started spewing many colorful expressions with my biggest point being that there is no such thing as an office anywhere in Afghanistan. Once I explained the soldier's work assignment a little better, the doctor that had signed the piece of paper told me that she had no concerns. I proceeded to our office and quickly typed out a simple three word document that read *Wash Rack Office*. I printed and slid the document into a plastic protector and expeditiously proceeded to the wash rack, where I attached it to the container door where we kept the materials staged. The specialist was incensed.

The next morning I was flying out to Kandahar, so I was not at our morning formation. Apparently after it was over, my specialist informed Sergeant First Class Bowen (my platoon sergeant) that she wasn't going to the wash rack that day and stormed off. He proceeded to follow her all the way to her tent and he entered the structure right after her. This is where the situation got hairy. My specialist proclaimed that he had walked in on her while she was undressed, even though he was probably only fifteen seconds behind her. She tried to escalate this to a higher level of command but it was rebuked quickly, as all the unit soldiers came out against her and no one believed that she could undress as fast as Superman in a phone booth. I was only gone two days, but by the time I returned, the tables had turned on the specialist and she was now pending disciplinary action for violating a direct order and making a false accusation. Her discipline was swift but tempered with a little bit of compassion as the book wasn't completely thrown at her. She did get sixty solid days of duty at the wash rack and after that, shockingly she never complained about the assignment again. In fact she didn't complain about much of anything during the rest of our time overseas, but she did make life challenging for a painful few weeks.

THE POLITICS

I WAS VERY LUCKY in the previous stories that my hands were completely clean in each of the soldier issues (maybe not entirely with the chief) but dealing with subordinates properly was always a stressor. I made sure that my i's were dotted and t's crossed in all areas concerning the soldiers, particularly discipline, as items tended to become very political. Afghanistan, as a whole, was way more political than I ever could have imagined. We always seemed to be adhering to a new flavor of the week. Our base rank structure was way out of whack and therein lay the majority of the issues.

The military has a dual rank structure, officers and enlisted. Officers make up about 20 percent of the Army, with Warrant Officers being a small fraction of this number. Enlisted soldiers make up the other 80 percent. As enlisted soldiers progress in rank, they can become non-commissioned officers. These non-commissioned officers pair with officer counterparts at each level of command. The pinnacle of the enlisted ranks is called a sergeant major and if they are in a command position, they are referred to as command sergeant majors. The first unit that you see a command sergeant major is in a battalion, which can encompass several hundred soldiers.

I laid out this introduction to begin to describe the rank structure on Bagram Air Field. Because we were in the in the beginning of the operation, we were exceptionally top-heavy. There was my battalion headquarters, a brigade headquarters, the division headquarters, and the corps headquarters all in one spot. That meant there were a lot of chiefs on a base that had just over a six-mile perimeter. And there weren't a whole lot of soldiers, not nearly enough for the sheer volume of leaders that we had. For the officers, this wasn't that big a deal, but for the senior enlisted, it goes against their military-engrained DNA. I have said many times in my career, I would much rather be at a place with sixty bored colonels than one bored sergeant major. This is because of how we are wired. As an officer, when we are not the biggest dog in the fight, we don't leave the fight to go find a smaller dog to fight. We don't make work for ourselves. On the other hand, senior non-commissioned officers are the stewards of the regulations and the standards. Their boredom will lead to stringent uniform and grooming inspections and the added *fun* of police call, a cleaning detail that resembles a chain gang where soldiers pick up trash around the base. While these are the right things to do in general, I have already mentioned the issues with showers and water, which made shaving a massive pain most of the time and led many of us to have electric razors sent to us from back home. That meant our faces weren't usually as clean-shaven as they probably should have been. The police calls were a whole other level of insanity, as we were in a war-torn country where everything that wasn't paved was mined. Any effort to pick up garbage off the beaten path had an inherent risk of loss of limb.

Luckily for me and my soldiers, our daily work area was on the back side of the base, so in a lot of situations, we were out of sight, out of mind. That didn't mean we were fully immune to the insanity, we just had to deal with it less. I guess that I should not have been surprised when the declaration came out that physical training (PT) tests were going to be required. There was only one legitimate road that could be run upon, but it also doubled as main artery for the base. I received the worst ass-chewing of my life on that road while driving past two joggers, one of them being our division commander who felt I was driving too fast past him. Mind you, this was during the workday (see paragraph above about time to kill) so I was a little indignant about a senior leader out jogging when the rest of us were working. That noted, jogging on the road was one thing, but having an entire unit shut the road down to run just seemed irrational. When you couple this with concerns about the air quality, it made the entire concept more ridiculous. But we didn't provide any pushback. Most of our soldiers were *prison buff* from working out or playing basketball during downtime, so we just took the opportunity to get them a good PT passing score and transportation across the base be damned.

While PT tests are regulatory (many times waived in combat theaters), the next dog and pony show that we were briefed on was not. Toward the end of the deployment, the decision was made that we would have a dining in (a formal banquet). This is usually reserved to be a formal military function with copious quantities of alcohol and our dress uniforms. It was done in an effort to lighten our mood and was meant to be a celebration, but when I got the uniform requirements for the event, which included silly things like wearing my canteen cup around my neck, mismatched uniform components, and several things worn inside out, I was anything but amused. I really liked our battalion headquarters, but this just seemed to go too far for me. It continued to hammer home the differing thought processing of this team and the structured nature of everything that they did. Dining ins in the States had silly uniforms so *by God* the ones in Afghanistan would also. I begrudgingly reviewed my dress requirements and got myself mentally prepared to be miserable, which didn't really give the event a chance. In all fairness, the event was anything but terrible, and once I let my guard down, I did enjoy myself a little bit. As a bonus, it did include a good meal, which was worth a lot of pain.

For everything I have talked about with military bureaucracy and politics, most resulted in a level of annoyance for me, but none had too negative an effect. That all changed during award preparation time. Our options at this time for awards were the Bronze Star Medal, the Army Commendation Medal, or a Certificate of Achievement. Each soldier would receive some form of award. My unit commander decided to put me, the first sergeant, and Sergeant First Class Bowen in for Bronze Star Medals. He composed an amazing award write-up for me, and I was flattered for the consideration, even though I wasn't sure if I really deserved it. With the awards submitted, I was called in to see Captain Pope a few days later, who informed me that my award would be downgraded, because, as he put it, "Lieutenants don't get Bronze Stars." The other awards would proceed onward. Whether I deserved the award or not was now irrelevant, as I believed that my efforts had equaled that of those that were receiving the award. I was seething that rank meant more than performance, especially as I was told mine was outstanding. As angry as I was when this information was conveyed to me, what came next was like a gut punch. We had been asked why my chief was not put in for a Bronze Star, which would be comparable with his rank. This was a man that nearly got fired and that I felt had actively worked against me. We had started to get along a little better, but this information tore the wound right back open. I am not 100 percent sure what words came out of my mouth when I was told this, but I am sure they were colorful and not appropriate for children to hear. I do remember that the last thing I said was that I would resign my commission as soon as we got home if that happened. I was ready to give up and quit. Not getting the award would sting, but that would have been a complete smack in my face. To Captain Pope's credit, he declined to nominate the chief, and although pushed some, he held his ground. He supported me and that made it hurt a little less. In the end, I did receive the Commendation Medal, but it was complimented with the write-up that CPT Pope submitted. Looking back now, that means more to me than the award itself.

PART V: THE LONG ROAD HOME

Home, where my thought's escaping.
Home, where my music's playing.
Home, where my love lies waiting.
Silently for me.
—Simon and Garfunkel

THE REPLACEMENTS

WHEN WE ARRIVED OVERSEAS the assumption was that it was only going to be a six-month deployment. The unit we replaced had only been there about five months and at this point mobilizations had not shifted to twelve months yet. That transition started while we were in country. With the build-up in Iraq, there were limited air resources and transportation assets to move people overseas, so getting replacement soldiers into Afghanistan wasn't a priority to anyone, except probably us. If someone had told me that I would have a one-year deployment going in, then I would have mentally locked-in for 365 days. Heading overseas after already having spent five months at Fort Lewis and fully expecting to only spend six month in country, every delay in leaving was exceptionally torturous. It appeared that with each week that passed, the date of our replacement unit's arrival would slip another week and we would add days to our countdown as we continued to just want to mark them off. The ultimate insult came on my twenty-third birthday in February when they basically told us that it was going to be at least another forty-five days before anyone would arrive. This *three hour tour* was never going to end. Now I knew how Gilligan felt. As shitty as it was, at least that lengthy delay recalibrated my expectations and actually made each day a little easier. We would just continue to do our mission to the best of our abilities, as we always did. I continued to check the air mobility website daily, which by way was the only thing I ever did that required a security clearance, as it was classified as secret. Finally, one fateful day, the replacement unit's name appeared, showing that they had dedicated transportation to get them overseas. Thank God!

This was the equivalent of cracking the Advent calendar open on the first day of December as a child. The big day was still a few weeks away, but it was now very much more plausible. The anticipation of leaving quickly came tempered by an *oh shit* moment. Our mindset completely shifted from one of daily survival to getting prepared to hand off the mission and to set this new team up for success, not that they really cared. I had previously exchanged a few messages back and forth with the new unit, but it seemed they weren't very interested in much of what I had to say. Giving them the benefit of the doubt, our notion was that they were just busy training and that we would touch base once they got on the ground. This made the days until their arrival feel like years, as the lack of communication made it feel more distant. At long last, the date of their arrival finally came. I remember distinctly going to the airfield to greet them getting off the airplane.

What I saw in the first thirty minutes of our replacements getting their boots on the ground foreshadowed what my next couple weeks would be like. I am not totally sure if their airplane unloading was meant to serve as a show of force, but that's what it resembled and it looked completely and totally ridiculous. The second the rear hatch of the airplane opened, the unit barreled out of the airplane in some odd formation, carrying all their large crew-served weapons (like mortars and big machine guns) as if they were going to toss them in position and start shooting people. At this point in time US service members had been in Afghanistan over a year, so we were not storming the beaches of Normandy looking to overthrow the enemy. Apparently, someone forgot to tell this to the new unit, or more likely they just weren't listening.

I had a good chuckle witnessing that train wreck, but I knew that I had to get it together to start the next phase of getting us home. I had been tasked to lead a small advance party back to Fort Lewis to coordinate our redeployment efforts, so I knew that my time was short in country. After herding all the cats off the airfield, we helped them get settled into their new living accommodations. We gave them a little bit of time to recover but needed to start our transition sooner rather than later. I was quite anxious to start handing over information to my new counterpart, as we had multiple projects in progress. Unfortunately, this was information that she really couldn't have cared less to receive. She was part of an active duty unit from Fort Bragg. The consensus from the unit was that they knew what they were doing and sure as hell weren't going listen to a reserve unit tell them how to run an active duty business. Ironically, nothing could be further from the truth for active duty units, as far as ammunition is concerned. Nearly all military installations that are equipped with ASPs are civilian-run and whether active duty or reserves, it is nearly impossible to complete real-world training for a unit. This arrogance was a flashback to the beginning of the deployment. If it had not been for the previous eight months in country with an amazing battalion headquarters from Fort Bragg, this would've seemed normal, but I was frankly shocked. I had busted my ass for eight months to get us where we were and I felt like all my efforts had been in vain. Everything we had put in place was going to change. Although we wore the same uniform, I felt again like I was not on their team.

My soldiers were also experiencing the same frustrations and all I told them repeatedly was to grin, bear it, and get over it. It's not what I wanted to say, but for once, the mature part of me had taken over. We just had to keep our eyes on the prize, which was that in a short period of time we were heading home, and their attitude wasn't going to change that.

The Army's transition plan was laid out pretty simply, it was a *right seat, left seat ride*. Basically, the incoming unit would operate in the right seat and observe the daily routine. Then, at a certain point, they would shift to the left seat and start leading the mission and we, the departing unit, would shift to the right seat and observe them. The assumption here is that the outgoing unit is the subject matter expert and the incoming unit, no matter how experienced, was the rookie. My time in the left seat was short and in keeping with the car analogy, our transition felt like the equivalent of an awkward twelve-hour car ride where no one speaks.

I felt that within days, we had been replaced, removed, and marginalized, and then something strange happened. My best guess is that the incoming commander strolled into a briefing with our battalion command team and touted his unit's greatness, but they hadn't actually learned the lay of the land. He acted as if he was a white knight, there to save the day, but instead looked more like an ass. He apparently couldn't describe the turnover plan between us because it didn't exist. Suddenly, two days before I was supposed to leave, the unit wanted to know everything that I knew. I was pissed off but obliged him with all that I had time to show him. Packing eight months of street smarts into two weeks would have been tough and pushing that into two days was impossible. During those insane two days, my replacement still found more time to point out all of my shortcomings than my successes. I got more and more frustrated, but soon it was over.

As I have matured and grown since I left Afghanistan, I have learned that no matter how much I prepare, someone who replaces me can always find fault in my processes and results. A true friend or teammate will focus more on what I did right than what I did wrong. This is why the Army moves people around a lot, infusing new ideas and energy into organizations to ensure that the envelope is always getting pushed and no one remains in the status quo. I fully expected our replacement unit to do better, because that's the way it works. The unit I replaced started first and ten at the one yard line (backed up to their own end zone). They got two first downs and got us to the twenty-five-yard line. We moved the ball to the fifty. Our replacement was set up to put points on the board. Points that they would get credit for but were a direct result of the work of several units. I didn't fully understand this during the transition process. Instead I was tense and guarded. I held a steadfast belief that we had done well no matter the criticism.

Forty-eight hours after the start of the last minute transition, it was my time to go. I headed to the airfield with one of my soldiers to begin our long journey home. With my departure I turned the page on that chapter in my life. I heard a rumor before we even got back to Fort Lewis that the replacement unit was struggling by trying to enforce rigid stateside standards in a war-like atmosphere. The devil on one of my shoulders wanted to celebrate their futility, but he didn't control me. In contrast, the angel on the other shoulder (and my brain and heart in the middle) only cared about the safety of all our supported units. I wished for everyone's success.

WELCOME HOME

FINALLY, I WAS ON MY WAY back to Fort Lewis. After the miserable months that I had spent there before heading overseas, the irony of my excitement to get back there was still not surprising. Since I was selected to lead the advance party back to the States to figure out the demobilization process, my sole focus was to get our soldiers out of the Pacific Northwest and back home as quickly as possible after they arrived. I previously spoke about leading the advance party to Afghanistan as well, which I decided meant one of two things: either my commander respected my abilities or he was trying to get rid of me. I always wanted to believe it was for the first reason, but my bull-in-a-china-shop mentality frequently had me teetering on insubordination, so there was room for a little doubt. Regardless of the reason, my sergeant and I sat at the airfield for what seemed like days waiting to get on a flight. I still had a bad taste in my mouth from the transition, but unlike my time spent reflecting how I got to Afghanistan on my flight into the country, my departure out of the country was mainly focused on the future. These contemplations also focused on seemingly insignificant things that crossed my mind, ranging from actually seeing trees and grass to getting used to walking wherever I desired again without the fear of stepping on a land mine.

We sat at the airfield for several hours, which for some reason is the military standard although not necessary at all. The only major milestones we had to complete were getting checked in and a customs check of our bags, where unlike in the US, someone physically went through everything that I had in my possession to ensure I wasn't leaving with contraband. After that, I threw my bags on a big metal pallet that was soon covered with a net. The only items I took on the plane were those that could fit in my cargo pockets.

Finally, after what felt like days, it was our time to board. Earlier I mentioned my military air travel getting to Afghanistan but wanted to take a moment to stress how it is different from civilian flights. When most fly commercially at home, herd mentality takes over. Most people that I have witnessed want to get on the airplane at their first available opportunity, anxiously waiting for their boarding zone to be called. This is not something I have ever cared to do, but many travelers rush to get on board to ensure they get proper space to store their carry-ons in the overhead bins so that they don't end up at their feet and therefore lose legroom. Boarding a military flight is significantly different. There are no carry-ons, and when you board a cargo plane to travel in the Army the first thing you do is get in your seat and strap in, but the second thing (sometimes concurrently) you do is start scouting what looks like the most comfortable place to sleep or lay down. I have slept in the beds of trucks and even on pallets of Tootsie Rolls. Basically everywhere in the cargo belly of the plane is fair game, except laying directly on the floor. I tried that once but woke up freezing shortly after getting up to elevation, as the only barrier between me and the freezing-cold air at 30,000 feet was the shell of the plane.

Before long we were airborne. I discovered my comfortable spot and I was knocked out for a long nap heading to Germany. Getting out of Afghanistan was easy except for the waiting time. I knew getting out of Germany was going to be a pain, since we did not have a dedicated trip home. We were basically acting like hitchhikers flying standby again, just trying to get someone to give us a ride. As soon as we arrived in Germany, we started scouting flight boards looking for a bird that could get us home. In what appeared to be our stars aligning, I immediately noticed a flight departing from Germany with a stop in Texas and a final destination of Fort Lewis. I couldn't believe our luck and I expeditiously got in line to request our names be added to the flight manifest. At this point, our stars fell out of the sky, as I was sternly informed that they would not allow us to be placed on that flight. My punch in the gut was not due to seating availability, but instead because there was a group of prisoners of war that were flying to the US on that plane and they were required to be segregated. I believe at this point I volunteered us to be blindfolded and gagged, but even that lighthearted request was instantly denied.

After several tries, we recalibrated our goal. We settled that we didn't care where we ended up at the conclusion of our next flight, just as long as it was the good ole USA. After a long day of waiting and begging, we finally found our transport, traveling with an air refuel team whose final destination was McGuire Air Force Base, New Jersey. At this point in my life I had never been to New Jersey, nor had I had a positive thought about New Jersey. In a few hours though, it would be where my welcome home was taking place and I was completely okay with that.

Our trip home was chauffeured by the Air Force and I was curious what that would mean. I had some previous notions that the Air Force lived a cushier life than the Army and my time in Afghanistan had done nothing to change that. As I waited in line to board the airplane, I was getting mentally ready to start my standard travel ritual, when something strange happened. Once I boarded the plane, I was pleasantly surprised to see standard aircraft seats— and that was just the tip of the Air Force iceberg. Before we had even reached our traveling altitude, the most amazing smell began to permeate the cabin. It turns out that airplane was also equipped with a full kitchen and the crew was making fajitas. Unfortunately, that delicious feast wasn't for us vagabonds. Instead I had to tear into my last military ration of the endeavor. I honestly don't think my tongue could have been any less disappointed.

After several flights hours spent questioning my military branch of service choice, our plane touched down on a spring evening in lovely New Jersey. We quickly gathered our bags and were told this was the end of our government journey, we would have to fly commercially the rest the way home. We researched and called the fastest shuttle we could get to the Philadelphia airport. At this point, we picked up a few other service members who had hitched a ride stateside as well, just with different final destinations. Once our group arrived at the airport, I was disappointed to learn that there were no flights that we could take that evening. That should not have been a surprise to me because it was about eight o'clock at night, but I was just anxious to get to my next stop. I was told to find a place to stay that night and to return first thing in the morning for a flight. After calling around to several hotels on the airport directory I finally found a place for all of us to stay, and I called for a shuttle. The ride back to the hotel was rather uneventful other than the older gentleman who was on the ride with us who discovered that we were on our way home, which by looking at us was certainly obvious. As we were piling out of the van, he gave me a fifty-dollar bill as the officer in charge to take the team out and buy them a drink. Most times nowadays, I would resist this gesture, but at that moment, I obliged. I could nearly taste the beer at this point. I can't remember what hotel brand we were staying at, but as we cascaded into the lobby, reeking of sweat and desert, I remember the young lady who checked us in asking if we had just gotten home from Iraq. Without thinking, I blurted out "nope—the other shithole." She looked rather startled and ask what I was talking about and I smugly told her that I meant Afghanistan. She proceeded to get more indignant with me because I had apparently insulted her homeland and the only reply I could give back to her was "you left the country for a reason." This may not have been the most mature thing to say at the moment, but I was high on the sweet smell of home, even if it was Philadelphia.

The receptionist may have been looking at that point to have a philosophical conversation about her motherland, but in my mind, there was no time to debate the conditions in Afghanistan. I had a mission and fifty dollars burning a hole in my pocket. Everyone quickly showered and got ready to head out for a night on the town. With eight months of mental preparation I can simply say that the night was long on anticipation and short on performance. We had a great night out, but everyone was jetlagged and an alcohol lightweight. We each retired rather early, knowing we had to catch a flight the next day, even though we did not know what time.

We arrived at the airport at six o'clock the next morning but were told due to flight cost the cheapest flight for the government didn't depart until four that afternoon, so for twenty dollars I had to spend ten hours in the Philadelphia international airport. To add insult to injury, it was Easter Sunday and, while not being overtly religious, it added a layer to my frustration. I offered to pay the twenty dollars out of pocket, but was told no. Easter Sunday aside, I decided to do what any good, young, single traveler would do with ten hours to burn and I started my day with Bloody Marys. Actually, I spent most of the day drinking and making random phone calls on the airport pay phones. I am fairly certain towards the end I was probably quite colorful. Not surprisingly, by the time I got on the airplane I sat down and passed out for the six-hour flight. It was easily the quickest flight I had ever been on as I only awakened when we touched down, with a hangover that was already creeping in. Even with my current haze and pain, I was elated to be back in Seattle. Our arrival was probably one of the most low-key military returns ever. There was no big welcoming committee for us, and that was acceptable as I still hated the place and didn't want any fanfare. In fact, our arrival was so barren that I had to use a payphone to call the girlfriend of one of my soldiers (he had met her while we were stationed at Fort

Lewis and their relationship surprisingly had survived) to come to the airport to pick us up. She was expecting us and quickly arrived at the airport. She took us straight to the base, where we checked in and found our billets. We settled in and tried to get some sleep, knowing the next morning would start the next phase of the struggle to get the unit home.

FORT LEWIS PART II: NO PRISONERS

I PREVIOUSLY TOLD THE STORY about running over my chain of command regarding a hotel stay at the very beginning of my mobilization. One might rationally deduce that I would have learned a lesson from this experience (hell, I claimed I did), but instead I put that approach on steroids as I began my task of demobilizing the unit. The objectives were simple: complete medical screening, turn in equipment and uniforms, and complete discharge paperwork for each soldier. I was laser-focused on getting my soldiers home, and I didn't care what it took. Fort Lewis took a vested interest in us, also. My unit had not been a typical mobilization for a reserve unit, but since we departed, Fort Lewis had become the scene of several unit mobilizations that were more traditional. We were the first unit that would be out-processing through the base, so they wanted to make sure everything was right. In fact, the senior civilian operations officer for the division, the military equivalent of a general, had given me his personal cell phone number and told me to call if I had any roadblocks. I should never have had to phone this friend, but circumstances started to change for me almost immediately. First off, Captain Pope got stuck in Afghanistan for a few extra days. The official story of his delay was a complication from transitioning military property on his hand receipt, but I suspected that he didn't want to deal with the bullshit he had previously experienced at Fort Lewis so had purposely made up an excuse to stay behind. Honestly, I couldn't blame him. Second, my previous brigade commander wanted to have a homecoming ceremony. I was dead set against this. Our schedule was going to be tight enough and spending the time to have a dog and pony show could have cost us an extra weekend. I instantly started looking for help, not wanting to pull the nuclear option yet. As my luck would have it, my reserve division headquarters had sent two representatives to aid me in getting the team home, a major and lieutenant colonel. I was eager to ask for their assistance, but as with many things, this option started with a lot of promise and ended with more frustration for me. I was told that they were there to help deal with O-5 (lieutenant colonel) issues and below, which was completely asinine. I wasn't afraid to escalate to the O-5 level, so why the hell could an O-5 not go one level up? My filter had long-since detached and I think my response amounted to something like "I'll handle my own O-5 issues. If you can't help me above that, then get out of my way." I'm sure my response was not quite that disrespectful, but I know they read between the lines of what I said. For me, this new revelation that I had hollow support further emboldened me. I would scorch the earth to get this unit home if I had to. As it turned out, I did talk to my civilian bigwig about the homecoming ceremony, but he advised me that we could work around it and it wasn't worth ruffling feathers. He committed to partner with me to get my team home without any additional delays.

Everything started simply. A formal flight was scheduled from Afghanistan for the unit and I had all our required activities scheduled, including what I felt was the pointless homecoming ceremony. It's not that I didn't feel like my soldiers deserved the added attention of a welcome home party. I just didn't believe these senior headquarters units had earned the right to celebrate with us after what they had previously put us through. I had reserved enough barracks to support the unit and had also filled each of the fridges in those barracks with beer in an effort to partially control the stupidity around everyone's new-found freedom. Upon their Tuesday evening low-key arrival, I told the soldiers that the expectation was that they would enjoy a beer or two and crash. I felt bad that they had just hit freedom and I subsequently locked them down, but I knew that this was the most expeditious way to accomplish the mission. I wanted to have them headed home in ninety-six hours. This regulated drinking may not have been their preferred method of celebration, but shockingly, it worked! About two hours after everyone arrived, all was quiet and I was feeling good.

The medical portion started rather smoothly as much as *hurry up and wait* can. My soldiers just wanted to sleep in their own beds, so they answered all post-deployment questions the right way, or at least the way that wouldn't delay them any further. In my subsequent deployments, many soldiers brought up all ailments during those medical screenings to ensure they received the future benefits for which they are entitled. This deployment was not the same. No one had any identified medical issues and by the end of day one, everyone had cleared our first gate.

This easy start to demobilizing brought about a sham confidence as we started phase two. Never in a million years did I think that turning in equipment and our uniforms were going to be a big deal, but then we started the process and things spoiled quickly. I started getting calls that they were trying to charge my soldiers for damage to their uniforms. Apparently, the person doing quality control of our uniform turn-in was not pleased that our uniforms had stains in the back of the neck and several holes throughout the uniforms. I quickly drove to our uniform turn-in thinking I could change minds quickly and that assumption could not have been farther from the truth. I got through the first concern rather expeditiously of the stains on the uniforms. I explained that the laundry group did not use soap to clean the uniforms and only hot water was used due to drainage and sewage concerns in Afghanistan. I further explained that we didn't have time to clean the uniforms, but I was sure that some Tide would handle the problem. I was feeling good that I had sold this well until we started talking about the holes in the uniforms. I provided what I thought was a simple explanation that we had spent countless days stringing concertina wire on our ASP perimeter for security reasons. The response I got was staggering. I was told that based off the duty descriptions for my soldiers that there was no reason for them to employ concertina wire, so they needed to pay for the damage to their uniforms. Once I realized that wasn't a joke, I became immediately infuriated by the stance of that stateside desk jockey on a power trip. I escalated to my civilian contact and pulled the nuclear lever. I don't have a clue what he did, but moments later all had been forgiven and gate two was cleared. That probably caused an additional layer of confidence that I didn't need, but at this point, I decided to schedule the unit's flight home. This was also the day of the unit's ceremony and with the power of the civilian behind us we easily finished early enough to accommodate that request. I must say that, for all my previous bitching about it, the ceremony was both respectful and reserved. Plus, as a bonus, it focused on my soldiers and not our Fort Lewis chain of command, which was one of my initial concerns. I was just happy it didn't add any time to our stay.

I woke up on that next morning feeling good about where we were. We tentatively had a flight home scheduled the next morning and I was feeling confident. Once all my soldiers finished, I could start my drive home and I was ready. All we needed was to have our DD-214s (discharge paperwork) cut for each of the soldiers. We headed to the out-processing station and the impediments started forming immediately. It was probably a combination of poor previous record-keeping and computer issues, but I wasn't all that concerned. Out-processing moved slowly, and we were trending to be done by about five in the afternoon, but apparently that was a major problem. I was told by the station chief that it was Friday and that the team out-processing us were finishing work by four and that we would have to come back Monday. I was told that the service members completing the work had been deployed to Fort Lewis and that they were being released at four o'clock to go home for the weekend to spend time with their families. This may have been the dumbest thing that I had ever heard in my life. How could they prioritize the soldiers mobilized to Fort Lewis above mine who had served overseas? I learned over subsequent deployments that I should have valued this out-processing team more, as they were filling their prescribed mission, but in that moment I didn't care. I protested but was told to get over it. At this point, I did all I knew how to do and dialed the phone yet again. I called my civilian contact and this time watched in live action as the phone rang in the distance and the civilian I was arguing with answered it. I didn't hear a single word that was exchanged, but I could see that the station chief did no talking but a lot of listening. He walked up as soon as it was over and declared that they would stay late to finish us. I am sure I was not very popular with him and the shit-eating grin on my face probably didn't help our relationship, but I seriously didn't care. It was time to go home.

I left the out-processing station and packed up my gear and filled-up my vehicle (I had paid to ship my personal vehicle to Fort Lewis while we were there). I completed one last confirmation on fight arrangements and bus transportation and returned to the out processing station to stalk my soldiers until completion. Once everyone was complete, I returned to our makeshift headquarters, did my final clearances, and grabbed two soldiers to begin what would become a fairly epic cross-country road trip.

AN EPIC CROSS COUNTRY ROAD TRIP

I HAVE SPOKEN PREVIOUSLY about our miserable time at Fort Lewis the first time and our ability as soldiers to adapt while I was in Afghanistan. These factors facilitated what would become the greatest road trip of my life. As I earlier mentioned, the ROTC mission only required about thirty workers, so we had roughly 130 soldiers that needed to have their idle time filled with stuff that did not involve punishing their livers. With no personal vehicles authorized for the mission, several soldiers were buying the cheapest vehicles they could find to help them get around. I had a new vehicle at home that I had recently purchased and feeling that I was too good for the $500 special everyone else was buying, I called my mom to help coordinate getting my vehicle shipped to me. To be clear, the irony of what I just wrote isn't lost on me, as I believed I was too hip for a cheap car but not too cool to ask my mom to help. The vehicle was a lifesaver for me. I used it to get around on post and the surrounding communities and also to provide a taxi service to many. As a bonus, when my unit further deployed overseas, the government picked up the tab to store it while I was gone. Upon my return to Fort Lewis, I was able to get my car out of storage without much issue, and it was critically important to getting around during our demobilization process.

The only detail I had to figure out now was how to get the vehicle home. While I had paid out of pocket to ship it to Washington state from West Virginia, I believed that since the Army had paid to store the vehicle that they would also pay to ship it back for me. At this point though, I discovered that the Army had used a loophole to store my vehicle while I was gone at their cost, but once I returned, I was going to be on the hook to pay to ship it back or to drive it back myself. In my mind this was the biggest *no brainer* of all time. Any consideration of risk was set aside even though I was jet lagged and needed to cover 2,500 miles in just over sixty hours. I determined that I would drive. I genuinely can't believe no one stopped me. Two of my soldiers volunteered to go with me to help drive, which in most normal circumstances would have raised red flags. The difference here was that at the end of our road trip we were heading our separate ways, so there was no reluctance due to fraternization concerns. Our mission was to leave on Friday late afternoon after being dismissed and we needed to be in Uniontown, Pennsylvania by Monday morning. All we had to do was make it 2,500 miles or so in sixty hours without the aid of GPS. This was 2003, and although I had previously owned a cell phone, none of us had reactivated service before our drive. So we fired up the MapQuest and set out about five o'clock in the afternoon on a fantastic voyage.

The two soldiers traveling with me had arrived back in the States on Tuesday night late and experienced about a ten-hour time change from Afghanistan, so they were still pretty severely jet lagged. I had been in the States a few extra days, but still had not adjusted. As with damn near everything associated with this deployment, the drive started with a lot of promise and nearly immediately sputtered out. We made it about 330 miles before we all hit a wall and were too exhausted to continue on. We gave up the fight and got off the highway in the biggest local city we could find on the map, Coeur d'Alene, Idaho. This was not nearly the progress we had expected. The first thing we did was head to the Taco Bell drive thru that began with significant anticipation and ended in an argument with a drive thru speaker. In what I perceived to be an area with tons of farmland and cows (and potatoes), Taco Bell was out of beef and steak. Seriously, cowboys and cows everywhere and I couldn't get beef, but I could get a side of potato products to go with my chicken. So we ordered our food and headed to a nearby off-brand hotel. As we pulled in the parking lot, I noticed some neon lights and an awning from just down the street. This could only represent one thing at this time of night—beer. We sent our negotiator into the hotel, who scored us a great deal on a room by I'm sure laying out the sob story of three wayward soldiers just trying to get home. While my negotiator was working, the other soldier and I were scheming. He had noticed the beautiful awning also and we were discussing how a couple of beers couldn't hurt. We parked the car, grabbed a few bags and headed to our room. Once there, we dropped our stuff off in the room, grabbed a spare key and announced that we were heading to the bar. Our negotiator looked a little perplexed by this decision-making because he thought we were exhausted. He decided to stay back and rest while the other soldier and I headed to get a beer.

The bar we walked into was like no place I had been before. I liken it to a Cheers for 1980s hair-band enthusiasts. As a special treat to us on this wayward night when we should have been sleeping, it was karaoke night. We were immediately greeted as we walked into the establishment with someone attempting to sing AC/DC. This prolific song rendition was followed by a daring Ozzy Osbourne tribute that left me questioning my decision to patronize this place. While I do like both of these artists, I had never witnessed them butchered via karaoke before. I imagined my ears going through stages from ringing, to bleeding, followed by long-term loss in the course of two short, shrieking songs. I was determined to soldier on and once I cut through the haze of the noise, I noticed a sign on the wall behind the bar that predominately advertised "$1 Molson's." This beautiful displayed changed my train of thought immediately and I suddenly didn't care about the hearing loss. We ordered our first round of beers and before we even got to our second, the third musketeer showed up. This was when the night started going downhill, as we proceeded to tear the night open, with beers and shots and butchering a few songs ourselves. All was going well during our impromptu drunken celebration until the bartender summoned us to bar and ask us to pull our pants down. Apparently, someone had shit all over the men's room bathroom and left their underwear behind. She declared that she wanted to make sure it wasn't caused by the outsiders in front of her. While this request was odd, the inebriating liquids inside us made this demand completely necessary in our minds. We obliged her mandate and quickly dropped our drawers. This was the easiest exam any of us had ever taken and we commemorated our success with a shot. I am not sure how any of us were still standing at this point, but we continued our celebration into the waning hours of the night. This is the time when bad decisions are generally made and this evening was no exception. We collectively decided that we needed to find a fun place to spend Saturday night and that we would pay for our poor decision-making on Sunday, which at that point was going to require a solid twenty-four hours in the car. We all agreed that if Coeur d'Alene was this great, we knew there would be other great memories to create somewhere else. Saturday night would be the culminating event for our deployment and we were ready for it. We closed the bar down that night and headed off to bed, buzzing about the future.

Fresh off probably about five hours of sleep, we woke early to continue our voyage. We started the day with a scarce continental breakfast and a driving choice: I-94 or I-90 to get cross-country. Channeling my childhood *choose your own adventure* books, I began to trace my finger across the computer screen, scouting which route gave us the best Saturday night option. Our decision ended up being I-90, and our destination was Gillette, WY, not for any reason other than the fact that it was the only place that sounded familiar. I believe deep down each of us knew that this was a terrible initiative, as Gillette was only about 700 miles away. This meant we were saving the last 1,500 miles for Sunday, but no one uttered a word of concern. We filled up the car and took off, sharing stories of our favorite part of our night before. All told, our drive was fairly uneventful and we arrived in Gillette early on Saturday evening. As we had done our previous night, we sent in our negotiator and storyteller to get us a good room deal, and once again, he was successful. We checked in, got cleaned up, and prepared for a wild night that we hoped would surpass our previous one. Gillette did not disappoint. The night started out tame at the hotel bar, enjoying dinner and drinks. Things escalated quickly as we met a group of locals who offered to take us to another bar. They cautioned us though that the other bar was a pretty rough establishment. Being cocky, we shrugged off this concern. There was no way that it could be worse than where we had been.

We crowded into some stranger's vehicle and began our drive getting mentally prepared for some version of *Roadhouse*. I was fully expecting to see Patrick Swayze's likeness at the door. Instead, we were greeted by nothing remotely intimidating. Granted, we were the only people in the bar without Stetsons, boots, and nice belt buckles, so we stuck out like sore thumbs. None of this mattered though because cowboys are damn patriotic. We had the time of our lives and shut the place down without a care in the world for the drive ahead. The night was everything that we envisioned it would be.

Sunday morning we were coming down. It was the exact opposite of the previous day's buzz. We had a long way to go and no one felt up to the arduous task. Luckily, one of my soldiers volunteered to take the wheel first to let the other two of us recover and by eight o'clock we were off. Someway, he got us through the first four hours and into South Dakota, where I took the wheel and never relinquished. This drive was much more stressful than the previous legs, as the radio station broadcasts were being frequently interrupted to convey messages of tornado warnings. Seemingly every fifteen minutes there was another one. I felt that our entire drive was the opposite of the movie *Twister*, as paranoia made it seem that we were dodging funnel clouds touching down all around us and not because we wanted them to. There was a feeling of relief when we crossed the Minnesota border, but that got awkward real quick. We stopped for gas at one of the first available stations and were confronted by a scene of dozens of young adults dressed in full gothic apparel. Nothing out of the ordinary happened, it just added to the peculiarity of this expedition. The remainder of drive took place without much incident, other than realizing the sheer size of driving across the city of Chicago. I dropped my soldiers off at their homes to get cleaned up and I headed to our reserve center. I arrived at about ten o'clock in the morning sporting three days growth of a beard and probably reeking. In that moment I didn't care. And in an instant, that swung 180 degrees, as the first person that I ran into at the unit was my brigade commander, a full bird colonel. While an uncomfortable conversation at first as I was trying to remain distant, it quickly turned positive. He was simply grateful for the mission we had just completed and he showered me with a lot of praise. It wasn't long before I zoned out. All I could think about was my last sixty hours where I had slept little and partied hard (twice), but still averaged traveling over forty miles each hour. I was smiling from ear to ear and he was oblivious to the whole thing.

MISSION COMPLETE

MY TIME BACK AT HOME station was brief. It consisted of a lot of paperwork and turning in equipment and also involved one last extravaganza to tell the unit goodbye. It was a night where there were multiple five-gallon buckets filled with beer, which paired well with lots of stories, high fives, and hugs goodbye. And then, practicing one final Army brainwashed moment, we decided sometime around midnight that it would be a good idea to start our last morning together with a long run. Previous to this, I had dreaded a 6am run while drinking at midnight. Never in a million years did I think I'd be the one gladly orchestrating this stupidity. And run we did. We closed the bar that night and everyone safely found their way home. The 6:00 a.m. formation surprisingly wasn't rough, because I think I was still drunk. This was a state that I remained in for at least the first three miles. Shockingly, no one puked and it was a great way to spend a few more precious minutes with my team. When it was over, I returned to the hotel, showered, checked out, and loaded up my car. The fact that my deployment was over had not fully sunk in and everything just seemed surreal. I headed to the unit for a brief period of time, and by lunchtime, I was gone. I spent the next three hours driving home, scrolling through radio stations, getting acquainted with several songs that I had never heard before. The hours passed like minutes, which was surprising since I was so anxious for it to all be over. And soon enough it was. I still vividly remember parking in my mom's driveway and walking to her front door, where I was greeted only by her and my sister. There wasn't any ballyhoo or a big party and that was exactly what I needed. As I looked in my mom's eyes, I saw a calming relief come over her. I know that I felt relief when I got back in the States, but nothing that could compare to the weight that I physically saw lifted from her shoulders in those few moments.

It had been sixteen months since it all started, and my emotions were nearly indescribable. The only word that easily comes to mind was *pride*. Had it not been for that aforementioned Fort Lewis battalion commander, my feelings would have probably been much different. When the call came to finally head overseas, we all assumed that was in the original plans but just hadn't been shared with us. That was absolutely not the case, as I found out during a brief conversation with my division contact at Fort Lewis as we were completing our final tasks before departing. We were all set to be at Fort Lewis for the entire year and it was the laboring and pleading of that commander that sold the Army on deploying us. He had the majority of one of his units overseas and he wanted them home and found us to be the way to get them out of there. I was shocked to find that a lieutenant colonel on active duty had that much power, but I truly wasn't fazed by it. As much as I hated him while we served under him, I would have told him thank you and probably hugged him for getting me overseas. That deployment helped define both me and our unit. Without it, I feel like it would have been a wasted year. It brought meaning to that mobilization. Without Afghanistan to hang my hat on, my entire experience would have involved drinking too much and killing a lot of time. Five months into my time at Fort Lewis, I was counting down the days until I could get out of the Army. Instead, this deployment set me up for a positive trajectory that led to the remainder of my military career that is twenty-two years strong. I also matured more in those eight months overseas than the preceding twenty-three years of my life.

To this day, I look back on my time in Afghanistan as the best of my career. I had amazing experiences with my soldiers, the locals, and an array of service members from other countries. We performed well as a team and left the country better than how we found it. There were many more goods than bads, more highs than lows, and it was absolutely my pleasure to serve.

PART VI: THE LEADERS THAT CHANGED ME

There goes my hero
Watch him as he goes.
There goes my hero
He's ordinary.
—The Foo Fighters

LIEUTENANT COLONEL BROADDUS

I WAS RECENTLY WATCHING a movie with my kids when the credits came on and my oldest son ask me if I liked to watch them. Generally I would say no, unless of course it is one of those films that has *Easter eggs* buried at the end that foreshadow future sequels or the great outtakes that often play at the end of many comedy movies. Viewed through another lens though, maybe my answer should be yes, as it memorializes the contributions of each of the cast and crew members to the overall final product. As I conclude my story, I now feel that leaving out my credits would be a tragic omission. I have purposely omitted the names of many characters in my personal odyssey, reserving that distinction for those that are wholly positive. That said, each member that I served with touched my career and life in some way. I would like to provide recognition to those whose impact I will never be able to fully quantify.

Lieutenant Colonel Matthew Broaddus was the commander of the logistics task force that I served under in Afghanistan. He had mobilized to Afghanistan as an active duty battalion commander from Fort Bragg, North Carolina. We were the only unit under his command that was not active duty and certainly not from Fort Bragg. After our initial experiences at Fort Lewis, it appeared that we were being thrown from the frying pan into the fire. Nothing could have been farther from the truth. His leadership was a 180 degree change to what we had originally experienced in our introduction to active duty. He was fair, treated all branches and services equally (there were times that it seemed that he even favored us), and did the right thing always, even though in my mind he didn't have to.

The welcome that we received from our peer units and the teamwork that we formed instantly breathed new life into my team. We deployed to Fort Lewis patriotic and passionate, and before long became glorified janitors and groundkeepers, driving cars that were older than many of our soldiers. While there is nothing wrong with those professions and vehicles, it wasn't the reason that we traveled 3,000 miles from home to serve our country. It was really hard for us. What a difference the new command made. Within a few short days in Afghanistan, we had our swagger back. At first, we were still guarded that the rug was going to be pulled from beneath us, but over time we grew to trust our new team and it felt so damned good to be a *real* soldier again. I attribute the majority of this to the stellar leadership of Lt. Col. Broaddus and the command climate that he built. He made us feel equal again.

Lt. Col. Broaddus spent countless hours with our unit just to learn who we were. He found value in discovering what each of our backgrounds were so that he could figure out how to best employ us. Yes, we were there to store and issue ammunition, but he understood the civilian skills that reserve soldiers bring to the table. He was running a task force that was building a base, so he valued our ability to help in other ways. I can't remember the exact quote that he told my commander about our unit, but it was something about how he enjoyed tasking us with non-standard missions because of the way we figured things out. We were in the Army but did not allow simple bureaucratic tendencies to get in the way of mission accomplishment. Even when our soldier screwed up by say looking at porn, he treated discipline the same as he would have for any soldier of any unit. When crappy details came up, he ensured that they were assigned evenly across the task force. He was a leader that I wanted to be.

After my terrible experience at Fort Lewis, Afghanistan was equally, if not more rewarding. Lt. Col. Broaddus is a major reason for that. He could have treated us the way we were treated at Fort Lewis, but that just wasn't who he was. Looking back, I think he saved my career from ending before it really got started, and I cannot express my gratitude enough for that.

MASTER SERGEANT WILKES AND SERGEANT FIRST CLASS BOWEN

MY NEXT CREDIT goes to a man who, as a non-commissioned officer, truly was the backbone of our unit. Sergeant First Class Arthur Bowen saved the day more times than I can count and I can't thank him enough. This doesn't mean that I was wasn't nervous in the beginning, as I'll explain below.

When I first arrived at my new unit to deploy, it had been just over two years since I received my commission and arrived at my first assignment as a second lieutenant. At the time, I had moved from one platoon to another in the same company to take on my new role. I knew little about the team I was joining, other than the fact that the civilian who ran the day-to-day business was a Vietnam Veteran and he was generally very intimidating. As I walked through his office door for the first time, Master Sergeant Don Wilkes smirked and the first words out of his mouth in my direction were: "I have socks older than you." To be fair, this was a true statement. In fact, I believe he had government-issued socks that he still wore that were older than me. This was both the first and last thing that was remotely abrasive that he ever muttered to me. After his initial response to me, M.Sgt. Wilkes became quite cordial, and over the next two years he became the most influential mentor that I had had to date in the Army. He adopted me as almost a son, and even invited me into his home where I met both his boys that were still in the house and his wife Tina, who was an amazing cook. Over time, I learned more about M.Sgt. Wilkes and the twenty-seven months of duty he performed overseas during the Vietnam War (in Korea, Japan, and Vietnam) in multiple functions, to include Air Rescue Recovery. I also learned of his follow-on career of distinguished service. I revered him.

As crazy as it may sound after that introduction, the most memorable experience that I had with M.Sgt. Wilkes was the day that I stood up to him—and more importantly, his reaction. We were in Egypt together a couple of short weeks after 9/11, participating in a training exercise that had gone dreadfully sideways. My packing list went from culturally sensitive civilian clothes for the pyramid tour to full chemical gear and a helicopter escort to the base. Needless to say, security for our operation was paramount and our contingency was tasked to help. So, M.Sgt. Wilkes, a small team, and I found ourselves setting up concertina wire around the base perimeter one night in the middle-of-nowhere Egypt. I can't recollect how the conversation started. All I remember from that evening was that there was a disagreement and at some point, I barked at M.Sgt. Wilkes about who was in charge. As soon as I realized what had come out of my mouth, I believe I probably turned completely pale. I had just yelled at one of my heroes, and worse yet, it was in front of others. To my surprise, M.Sgt. Wilkes' reply was not one of anger. He simply smiled from ear to ear and told me I was going to be alright. At that moment, he picked me up from my lowest low and lifted me up. M.Sgt. Wilkes' affirmation during that encounter was a monumental moment for me, as I feel like it was the day that I arrived as a leader. If I had his seal of approval, I knew that I could do anything.

For this deployment, I was confident but tepid. With this new unit, I knew I would be losing my previous safety net and it scared me a little. I was like a young animal being kicked out into the wild on my own. My fears were certainly not put to rest when I arrived at the unit to be greeted by my over-ranked civilian in charge and the current platoon sergeant. I had been told that the platoon sergeant would not be deploying with the unit due to medical conditions, and that his time in charge was only temporary. He was being replaced by another outsider from the organization. The day that Sergeant First Class Bowen walked into the unit I had no idea what to expect. Within moments of his arrival, he immediately made an impact on our situation. The first interaction that I remember him having was with the civilian. Sgt. First Class Bowen asked if there was coffee brewed and the civilian replied that he only drank tea. I believe his abrupt response was something along the lines of "what kind of man doesn't drink coffee?" With a combination of shock and outrage the civilian informed Sgt. First Class Bowen that he was a colonel in the reserves. Sgt. First Class Bowen's reply introduced me to his catch phrase: "I don't give a fuck." This was followed by "you're a civilian that works for me today." I think I was both in disbelief and elated that I had someone to fight this battle with me. That said, Sgt. First Class Bowen's struggle to gain control of the unit was much harder than mine. He had to wrestle everything away from the previous platoon sergeant, while helping me fight the civilian who frequently made decisions that bordered on the unethical. A prime example of this was the meal contract that he set up for our time at home station before we left for Fort Lewis. He had arranged our contract at a restaurant that his daughter had previously worked at during college and he knew the owners. This normally would not have raised any red flags being in a small town, until the soldiers complained to Sgt. First Class Bowen about the arrangement he had set up in addition. Each soldier got an allowance at the restaurant for their meal that was a certain dollar figure, but the civilian had declared to everyone that they could only spend two dollars less than that amount in order to leave a mandatory gratuity for the server. The kicker of it all was that the receipts would come to the unit for the full amount. I was surprised that the soldiers had not previously brought this up to me but really floored when I found out what was happening. Being an outsider to the organization, Sgt. First Class Bowen had some previous connections, and after he dropped a few names with our civilian, our meal problem went away. Much the same way that our hotel situation formed a bond between the soldiers and me, the meal changes had the same impact for Sgt. First Class Bowen. We were starting to gel together and we had the total support of our soldiers, so things were very good.

Once we got to Fort Lewis, our bond only grew stronger and Sgt. First Class Bowen and I worked tirelessly as a team together. We each supported the other well, and when it was time to head to Afghanistan, we were as solid as we had ever been. Little did I know going overseas that Sgt. First Class Bowen would end up being the glue that would hold it all together. As I previously mentioned, my relationship with my ammunition chief was fractured, and while this didn't lead to many issues running the day-to-day business of the ASP, we were having factional issues from a leadership standpoint. The company commander stood by me and the first sergeant leaned to support the chief more, both probably simply because of personal relationships. Sgt. First Class Bowen turned into our intermediary during many stressful situations and basically held the unit together while we were hashing out our differences, which we eventually did. Throughout the entire process, Sgt. First Class Bowen was phenomenal. He didn't take sides and helped share his seasoned opinions that held a lot of gravity with both of us. The best part of the entire situation was that he shielded the soldiers from it, which could have caused a lot more problems. His coolness under fire can't be overstated and again, I could probably never thank him enough.

M.Sgt. Wilkes taught me how to lead and Sgt. First Class Bowen taught me the right ways to lead. The Army's model of pairing seasoned non-commissioned officers with young lieutenants got everything right and has molded my career.

CAPTAIN POPE

I AM MORE THAN 49,000 WORDS into this tale of one of the most influential parts of my life, and I have saved the best for last. Captain James H. Pope, to this day, is an enduring substantial figure in my life. My relationship with him started during this excursion where he was my commander, my mentor, and my friend, but has sewn us together for forever. I joined his tenured and close-knit team as an outsider who had simply volunteered to answer the call (or was in the wrong place at the wrong time, depending on how I look at it). Hell, I was even the odd man out as it related to reverence behind my last name. Besides Capt. Pope, two of the other platoon leaders that I mobilized to Fort Lewis with were Lt. King and Lt. Lord. *Lt. Warner* just doesn't have the same ring to it. That said, within six months after our first meeting, Capt. Pope believed in me and gave me one of the greatest opportunities of my life: a chance to lead America's sons and daughters into war in a conflict that we all believed in.

So who was this larger than life figure? To answer simply, he was a tech dork from Alabama who at times spoke in languages I did not understand. His primary civilian occupation was as a computer programmer who had worked on multiple government projects where his billing rate per hour was more than I had ever made in a single day. He was married with no kids and had an uncanny musical appreciation for Abba and Bella Fleck.

These are all superficial narratives for Capt. Pope that hardly make him appear to be the second coming of Superman. And they certainly do not do justice to the true chronicle of this incredible officer, leader, and human being. To understand that fully, you would have to peel back a couple layers to discover that he was also stubborn, compassionate, loyal, resilient, and the most selfless person that I have ever met.

I have already discussed a few times our struggles at Fort Lewis and the burden on our unit that was mainly shouldered by James Pope. I honestly have no idea how he kept it all together. Capt. Pope had to be a unifying voice in front of his soldiers who were in a terrible situation, even though he was getting kicked repeatedly in private. Combine this with the extreme financial toll that the deployment took on him from a personal standpoint and one could easily ascertain that it would have been simple for him to fail. This is where the stubbornness came in. For most, being stubborn is not always viewed highly, but in this situation, it drove Capt. Pope. He believed in the mission, his duty, and his soldiers, and everything else was just distracting noise.

We would have followed him to the ends of the earth, and being in Afghanistan, it really felt like we did. This austere environment is where we really hit our stride and began to mimic our leader. His sacrifice and selflessness started to resonate in each of us, and while we did have some struggles and what the Tuckman Model would call an exceptionally long storming phase in our team development (truth be told, we stormed a second time when we got to Afghanistan), we ended the deployment as a cohesive unit.

I believed in Capt. Pope so much that after only about sixteen months at home, he called and ask me if I would be willing to deploy with him again. I think he knew the answer before he called, because I would have mobilized to hell to fight the devil with him if he asked.

And within a few weeks, I was gone. I was ready to serve my country again, knowing he would be leading from the front. That's all the reassurance I needed. Ironically, my second deployment ended up being a lot like hell. But that's a story for another day . . .

ACKNOWLEDGMENTS

WRITING THIS BOOK was one of the most personal things that I have ever done in my life and also a huge stretch for me, but I wanted to make sure that I left a voice behind. I have mentioned four incredibly important leaders in my military career in this book that I could not have survived without. I want to thank them once again. As for the rest of my career, I can't begin to list the people that have impacted me, as it would take up the next several pages and I would undoubtedly leave someone out. That considered, I'd like to personally thank all the brave men and women that I have served with. It has been an honor.

I want to thank my immediate family! From the weekly care packages, to the letters and emails, you have kept me connected to home, even when I was far away, and I thank you.

Lastly, to Betsy and the kids (Porter, Nash, Archie, Ellis, and Kora): I love you all more than I can ever describe. I want to say thanks for bringing so much added meaning to my life.

CPSIA information can be obtained
at www.ICGtesting.com
Printed in the USA
LVHW031309010421
683210LV00009B/479